Antony Worrall Thompson

fast family food

Antony Worrall Thompson

fast family food

PHOTOGRAPHS BY DEIRDRE ROONEY

MITCHELL BEAZLEY

To the Malahide Shiels, a family in perfect harmony

Fast Family Food
Antony Worrall Thompson

An Hachette Livre UK company
www.hachettelivre.co.uk

First published in Great Britain in
2008 by Mitchell Beazley
An imprint of Octopus Publishing Group Ltd,
2–4 Heron Quays, Docklands, London E14 4JP

ISBN 978 1 84533 2884
A CIP record for this book is available
from the British Library

Commissioning Editor Rebecca Spry
Art Director Tim Foster
Designer Nicky Collings
Photographer Deirdre Rooney
Prop Stylist Isabel De Cordova
Home Economist Sara Lewis
Project Editor Georgina Atsiaris
Copy Editor David Tombesi-Walton
Proofreader Jo Murray
Production Lucy Carter
Index Diana LeCore

Set in Agilita and Absara

Printed and bound by Toppan Printing
Company, China

contents

Research tells us that eating round the table as a family is becoming a thing of the past. To me, the kitchen or dining table is where it's at: it's the family boardroom, where decisions are made, problems solved, manners taught and communication skills developed.

These days, many activities within a family are often fragmented: Dad taking son to football or rugby, Mum taking daughter swimming or riding. Time is rarely on the side of joint participation. How many parent-teacher evenings, prize-givings or carol services have I missed because of work? Too many. However, at least once a day, I try to get everyone around the table for a bite to eat and a good old natter.

Although time is in short supply, I would urge you to cook your meals from scratch to enable your children to enjoy a healthy and balanced diet. I have used ready meals on occasions, especially when my children are left in the care of a babysitter, but looking at the sugars, salts, fats and additives many contain, I feel I am doing my children a disservice.

Cooking from scratch doesn't need to take long, as I'm about to show you. I've got a feeling that you're going to say, 'But it's easy for you – you're a chef! It'll take me twice as long.' Well, my family tested cooking many of these recipes and found they could cook them in the time indicated. Like most things in life, if you want to cook well, the key is good organization, and that means good preparation. Throughout the book, the word 'meanwhile' appears regularly in the recipe methods; please don't ignore it, since it is used to mean that while you're simmering, boiling, frying, etc, you should be moving on to the next task, so that two stages are happening at the same time.

Cooking is all about confidence. Don't overextend yourself. If you want to cheat a little (and Delia has made it all the rage), please feel free. Use that ready-prepared veg, buy some ready-made sauces – I don't care too much. The priority is for you to get into the kitchen, to cook simple, good, honest family food and to forget about trying to cook like a chef. Just concentrate on being a real parent.

That said, I've resisted the temptation to include recipes even faster than those in this book because I really want you to cook rather than open too many packets or cans. However, to help, under many recipes I've given you a handy hint, which often contains a little cheating advice.

Finally, while the health aspect of family food is important, it should never be the overriding factor. Children and adults alike must be allowed to enjoy their food without the food police hovering over their shoulders tut-tutting every time they eat something naughty. Health is about balance and about eating a wide range of ingredients with no food groups excluded. As a parent, you know whether your children are overweight or fighting fit, and you can therefore decide whether to give them that pudding or that extra bowl of chips. But always remember: if you are eating more calories than you're burning off through exercise or activities, you are going to get fat. Simple fact, simple cure.

The main thing is to enjoy my food. This is real family food produced quickly; you won't find any towers, swirls of foam or reduced balsamic vinegar, and I haven't used any ingredients that you can't buy in the supermarkets, either. I hope you'll enjoy my book and discover deliciously simple food. I've enjoyed writing it, I've enjoyed preparing the recipes and I've enjoyed eating the results. Go wild in your kitchen.

brunch

Brunch is the perfect meal for lazy weekends. You get up late, too late for breakfast, but you're really hungry and it's too early for lunch. So brunch it is, and my selection of dishes means that you don't need to spend hours in front of the stove.

Apart from my Cheesy Muffin Brunch Buns, I haven't gone for American food. I find all that maple syrup and those pancakes too much for the waistline. For this chapter, I'm looking for food that is reasonably healthy while still being moreish; delicious food that can be knocked up in a flash and that will sustain you for much of the day.

Most of the influences come from Europe, and many of the dishes are also suitable for a snack, lunch or supper. Will the children enjoy them? Some will, some won't, but one must never be afraid of giving kids new taste experiences.

Eat with your children and enjoy your food openly. Children are born mimics, so if you like your food, they will probably like it too. Getting your children to be adventurous with food relies heavily on trust, so eat as a family, eat the same food and engage in conversation.

Porridge is a must on a breakfast regime, offering a low GI (Glycaemic Index) rating and keeping you sated until lunchtime. The downside is that it can often get a bit dull. Try this recipe to up the excitement ante!

Porridge with Apples and Crunch

Timetable: from start to table in 20 minutes
Preparation 10 minutes | Cooking 10 minutes

For the compote, combine the apples, sugar, cinnamon, vanilla and water or juice in a small saucepan. Bring to the boil and simmer for 10 minutes, stirring from time to time. Remove the vanilla pod.

Next, combine all the porridge ingredients in a non-stick saucepan and bring to the boil. Reduce the heat and simmer for about 5 minutes, until thickened; if the mixture is too thick, add a little more milk.

Divide the porridge between four warm bowls, top with some warm apple compote and sprinkle with the crunchy muesli. Drizzle over some honey if you wish.

Antony's tip Play with different fruits using the same recipe – pears, apricots, red fruits, figs… the choice is yours.

Serves 4

FOR THE COMPOTE

2 Cox or Granny Smith apples, peeled, cored and thinly sliced

40g (1½ oz) caster sugar

Pinch of ground cinnamon

Half a vanilla pod, split lengthways

60ml (2fl oz) water or apple juice

FOR THE PORRIDGE

115g (4oz) porridge oats

600ml (1 pint) full-fat or semi-skimmed milk

2 tbsp soft light-brown sugar

Pinch of salt

TO SERVE

4 tbsp of your favourite muesli

A drizzle of honey (optional)

Asparagus for Brunch What can I say about this simple dish except that it offers a lovely combination of flavours?

Timetable: from start to table in under 25 minutes
Preparation 10 minutes | Cooking 13 minutes

Preheat the oven to 180°C/360°F/Gas 4. Place the tomato halves in a large frying pan, sprinkle with garlic, thyme, salt and pepper, and drizzle with a little olive oil. Cook over a medium heat for 5 minutes, then pop in the oven for 8 minutes.

Meanwhile, bring a large pot of salted water to the boil, cook the asparagus for 4 minutes, then refresh under cold water. Take bundles of four asparagus sticks and wrap them in one rasher of bacon. Cut the other four rashers into lardons. Pop the asparagus bundles and the lardons into a large oiled griddle or frying pan and cook until the bacon is brown, turning regularly.

Place the rocket in a bowl with the bacon lardons, the remaining oil and the balsamic vinegar, and season with black pepper. Arrange the salad in the centre of each of four plates, top it with two halves of roasted tomato, straddle the tomatoes with an asparagus bundle, then scatter with Parmesan flakes.

Serves 4

4 large vine tomatoes, halved horizontally

1 clove garlic, finely chopped

1 tsp soft thyme leaves

Salt and pepper

3 tbsp extra virgin olive oil

16 sticks of asparagus, trimmed

8 rashers of dry-cured back bacon

2 handfuls of rocket

2 tsp balsamic vinegar

25g (1oz) Parmesan flakes

This all-in-one breakfast/brunch dish encompasses many elements of a fry-up but in a healthier fashion. It's a dish that can be prepped up the night before, so all you have to do in the morning is pop it in the oven.

Breakfast Tomatoes

Timetable: from start to table in under 30 minutes
Preparation 12–15 minutes | Cooking 12–15 minutes

Preheat the oven to 180°C/360°F/Gas 4.

Cut 1cm (½ in) off the top end of each tomato and scoop out the seeds, retaining the 'lid'. Sprinkle each tomato with a little salt and place them cut side down to drain.

Meanwhile, heat the olive oil in a frying pan, add the bacon and fry until starting to crisp – about 3–4 minutes. Next, add the mushrooms and cook quickly for 3–4 minutes; finally, fold in the chives and season with black pepper.

Spoon the mixture into the tomatoes, making them no more than half full, then place the tomatoes on a lightly oiled baking tray. Crack an egg into each tomato, then dot with a little butter and season lightly. Replace the tomato lids and cook for 12–15 minutes, depending on how you like your eggs. Timing depends on the size of the tomatoes and the eggs.

Antony's tip I find a melon baller the best gadget for removing the seeds – just be careful not to puncture the skins.

Serves 4

4 large, firm beefsteak tomatoes

Salt and ground black pepper

1 tbsp olive oil

6 rashers smoked streaky bacon, diced

125g (4oz) button mushrooms, quartered

1 tbsp snipped chives

4 free-range eggs

25g (1oz) unsalted butter

Tomato Cream on Toast with Crispy Bacon

There's something quite satisfying about tomatoes and bacon oozing with cream. It's the perfect breakfast food for an indulgent, decadent weekend.

Timetable: from start to table in 25 minutes
Preparation 10 minutes | Cooking 15 minutes

Place the tomatoes, cut side down, in a large frying pan with half the oil and the butter. Cook for 8 minutes over a medium heat, then turn the tomatoes over and cook for a further 5 minutes, until the tomatoes have softened and caramelized. Season with salt and black pepper. Pour the cream over the tomatoes, then add the chives. Bring to the boil and allow to bubble for 2 minutes.

Meanwhile, cook the bacon in the remaining oil until crispy – about 7 minutes – and toast the bread.

Place the toast on four warm plates, top each slice with bacon, then spoon over the tomatoes with their creamy juices.

Antony's tip I love the fat in streaky bacon because it gets nice and crispy. However, if fat is not your thing, feel free to use back bacon instead.

Serves 4

8 medium-sized ripe tomatoes, halved horizontally

1 tbsp good olive oil

25g (1oz) unsalted butter

Salt and ground black pepper

150ml (5fl oz) double cream

1 small bunch of chives, snipped

8 rashers of smoked streaky bacon

4 slices of country bread

Grown-ups occasionally need a reminder of simpler times. In food terms, such feelings lend themselves to comfort eating, and things on toast come to mind: baked beans, scrambled eggs, tomatoes and bacon… or these satisfying spicy mushrooms.

Spicy Mushrooms on Toast

Timetable: from start to table in 30 minutes
Preparation 10 minutes | Cooking 20 minutes

In a frying pan over a moderate heat, cook the onion, ginger, garlic and chilli in the two oils until the onion is soft – about 8 minutes.

Increase the temperature, add the mushrooms and cook for 5 minutes. Add the wine, honey and ketcap manis, and cook for a further 5 minutes. Season to taste.

Meanwhile, toast the bread. With a slotted spoon, scoop the mushrooms out of the pan and place them on the toast.

Boil the juices remaining in the pan over a high heat until no more than four tablespoons remain. Pour these juices over the mushrooms, then scatter with spring onions, coriander and mint, and top with a good dollop of yogurt.

Antony's tip Freezing the ginger makes it easier to grate.

Serves 4

1 onion, finely diced
1 tsp grated ginger
1 clove garlic, finely diced
1 chilli, finely chopped
1 tbsp sesame oil
2 tbsp vegetable oil
325g (12oz) button mushrooms, quartered
150ml (5 fl oz) dry white wine
1 tbsp clear honey
2 tbsp ketcap manis
Salt and ground black pepper
4 slices of granary bread

TO SERVE

4 spring onions, sliced
1 tbsp chopped coriander
1 tbsp chopped mint
4 tbsp Greek yogurt

Open-Faced Cheese and Ham Toasties

Show me a child, apart from a vegetarian one, who doesn't enjoy a cheese-and-ham toastie. In an effort to reduce processed carbohydrates, I've cut out the top slice of bread. This makes the dish a knife-and-fork job, but it's a good snack, nevertheless.

Timetable: from start to table in under 15 minutes
Preparation 10 minutes | Cooking 3–4 minutes

Toast the bread on one side only, then butter the untoasted side. Lay a slice of ham on each slice, and follow that with two slices of mozzarella and a good twist of black pepper.

Combine the grated cheese with the cream (if using), mustard and Worcestershire sauce, then spread this mix over each sandwich, making sure all the edges are covered. Place it under the grill and cook until bubbling and golden. Serve immediately.

Antony's tip As the children's taste buds get more sophisticated, you can play around with different cheeses, such as a blue or a Camembert. Some chutney or pickles go well under the ham, as do slices of tomato.

Serves 4

4 slices of country rustic bread, brown by preference

40g (1½ oz) unsalted butter

4 slices of thick-cut ham

1 ball of cows' mozzarella, cut into 8 slices

Ground black pepper

115g (4oz) Emmental or Cheddar cheese, grated

2 tbsp double cream (optional)

2 tsp Dijon mustard

1 tsp Worcestershire sauce

Hot Stuffed Croissant

There are times when all I fancy is a quick sandwich. This hot croissant stuffed with melting Brie over watercress and sliced pears is a lovely treat and the perfect way to fuel up on energy-giving carbohydrates.

Timetable: from start to table in under 20 minutes
Preparation 10 minutes | Cooking 8 minutes

Preheat the oven to 180°C/360°F/Gas 4.

Slice the croissants horizontally in two.

Pick the watercress into small florets and arrange on the bottom half of the croissants.

Slice each pear in half lengthways, then each half into six slices. Divide these slices between the four croissants. Top the pears with slices of Brie. If you wish, you can cut off the Brie crust, but this isn't necessary. Season with a little salt and ground black pepper.

Top with the croissant lid, pop into the oven and heat through until the Brie is meltingly gooey and soft – about 8 minutes.

Antony's tip Eating a bag of watercress is said to be a good cure for a hangover!

Serves 4

4 butter croissants
1 bunch of watercress
2 pears, peeled and cored
225g (8oz) ripe Brie cheese, sliced
Salt and ground black pepper

These doughy little numbers will surprise with all their flavour, and they're delicious hot or cold.

Cheesy Muffin Brunch Buns

Timetable: from start to table in 35 minutes
Preparation 10 minutes | Cooking 25 minutes

Makes 12 muffins

450g (1lb) self-raising flour
40g (1 ½ oz) unsalted butter
450ml (15fl oz) buttermilk
2 eggs
2 tbsp sun-dried tomato pesto
85g (3oz) grated Emmental cheese
2 tbsp snipped chives
½ tsp sweet paprika
Salt

Preheat the oven to 190°C/375°F/Gas 5. Lightly butter and flour a 12-hole muffin tray.

Tip the self-raising flour into a bowl, then cut the butter into the flour using two knives or your fingertips. Stir in the buttermilk and eggs to form a soft, slightly wet dough. Lightly fold in the pesto, cheese, chives, paprika and a pinch of salt. Divide the dough between the 12 muffin holes.

Place in the oven and cook for 25 minutes. Allow to rest before turning them out onto a wire rack.

Mini Pea, Ham and Cheese Frittatas

Get your children to help you make this nice little brunch-style dish. The frittatas can be served hot or at room temperature, which makes them perfect for the lunch box.

Timetable: from start to table in 25 minutes
Preparation 10 minutes | Cooking 15 minutes

Preheat the oven to 180°C/360°F/Gas 4.

Whisk the eggs and cream to emulsify, then fold in the Emmental, herbs and peas. Season.

Lightly oil 12 holes of a muffin or Yorkshire pudding tray. Line each hole with the ham – don't worry if the slices are too big. Spoon the egg mixture onto the ham. Break or crumble the ricotta into small pieces and dot the top of the egg mix with it. Place in the oven. Cook for 10–15 minutes, until the egg mix no longer wobbles.

Allow to cool slightly before turning out. Serve with salad or grilled tomatoes.

Antony's tip This is a dish that you can have great fun with: vegetarians can omit the ham and choose from a wide range of cheeses, herbs and vegetables. Feel free to use whatever grabs your fancy, as long as you stick to the basic egg-and-cream mixture.

Serves 4

6 free-range eggs

125ml (4¼ fl oz) double cream

55g (2oz) grated Emmental cheese

1 tbsp snipped chives

2 tsp snipped dill or tarragon

85g (3oz) frozen peas, defrosted

Salt and ground black pepper

6 slices of cooked ham, cut in half

85g (3oz) ricotta cheese

TO SERVE

A fresh salad or grilled tomatoes

Elizabeth David probably did more to educate British palates than any other writer in the past 100 years. I met her only three or four times cooking for her twice, but the impression she made on me will survive throughout my cooking lifetime. This recipe is inspired by one of the first dishes I attempted from her cookbooks.

Piperade

Timetable: from start to table in 30 minutes
Preparation 10 minutes | Cooking 20 minutes

In a frying pan cook the onion, garlic and thyme in the olive oil until soft. Add the peppers and cook for 10 minutes. Add the tomatoes and cover the pan.

Cook until all the ingredients are soft and combined. (This dish could be prepared in advance up to this point.)

When ready to eat, pour in the eggs and cook as you would scrambled eggs. Season to taste, and serve hot with slices of ham on the side.

Antony's tip Seed the peppers by slicing them vertically from one side of the stem to the other; break them apart, and the seed core should pop right out. Then cut away the bitter membranes, before slicing the pepper from the flesh side, which is easier than slicing from the skin side.

Serves 4

325g (12oz) onion, finely sliced

1 clove garlic, finely diced

1 tsp soft thyme leaves

3 tbsp good olive oil

1 red pepper, seeded and cut into thin strips

1 green pepper, seeded and cut into thin strips

4 tomatoes, peeled and chopped

6 eggs, beaten

Salt and ground black pepper

TO SERVE

175g (6oz) cooked ham, thinly sliced

Baked Eggs with Potted Shrimps
This dish is made with a famous 'fishy product' that has been overlooked in our constant search for more off-the-wall items.

Timetable: from start to table in under 15 minutes
Preparation 5 minutes | Cooking 7–10 minutes

Preheat the oven to 190°C/375°F/Gas 5.

Butter four china ramekins, using the butter from the shrimps. Divide the shrimps into four portions and push them into the ramekins. Season the cream and pour over the shrimps.

Break an egg into each ramekin and place the ramekins in a small baking dish half-filled with hot water. Bake in the oven for 7–10 minutes, depending on how firm you like your eggs.

Serve immediately with buttered-toast 'soldiers'.

Antony's tip Those who don't like seafood can substitute the potted shrimps with diced ham and grated cheese.

Serves 4

2 x 25g (1oz) tubs potted shrimps
Salt and ground black pepper
175ml (6fl oz) double cream, heated
4 large free-range eggs

Chinese Crispy Fried Eggs with Oyster Sauce
Fancy something completely different from your normal breakfast offerings? I learned this recipe from a great Australian chef, Kylie Kwong.

Timetable: from start to table in 10 minutes
Preparation 5 minutes | Cooking 5 minutes

Heat the oil in a wok until the surface starts to shimmer. Break two eggs into each of four bowls. Meanwhile, toast the bread.

Pour one bowl of eggs into the oil, followed by another bowl. Allow the eggs to become crisp – this will take about 90 seconds. Remove the eggs, set aside and keep warm. Repeat with the other two bowls of eggs. Once you've removed the eggs, tip the oil into a bowl (this can be reused once cooled and strained), then return all eight eggs to the wok to crisp up, making sure to keep the yolks soft.

Place two eggs onto each slice of toast, drizzle with oyster sauce and a little chilli oil (if using), and sprinkle with the spring onions, chilli some coriander leaves and white pepper.

Antony's tip I never thought I'd enjoy crispy eggs, but these are excellent. You can try them drizzled with other Chinese sauces too.

Serves 4

330ml (12 fl oz) vegetable oil
8 free-range eggs
4 slices country bread
2 tbsp oyster sauce
½ tbsp hot chilli oil (optional)

TO SERVE
4 spring onions, finely sliced
1 red chilli, finely chopped
Coriander leaves
White pepper

My friend Ching He-Huang did a smashing dish in a similar vein to this on *Daily Cooks*. This is easy, lovely and full of flavour – you'll love it!

Breakfast Rice with Sweet Prawns

Timetable: from start to table in 25 minutes
Preparation 10 minutes │ Cooking 15 minutes

For the rice, heat the oil in a large wok until almost smoking, then tip in the eggs and stir continuously until set – about 1 minute. Remove and set aside.

Put the bacon in the wok and fry until crispy. While the bacon is cooking, microwave the rice according to the manufacturer's instructions.

Meanwhile, add the onion to the bacon and cook for 3 minutes; tip in the rice and peas, and cook until hot. Roughly chop the egg and add to the rice, along with the soy sauce and sesame oil. Season with white pepper.

Meanwhile, for the prawns, heat the oil in a large frying pan or another wok. Throw in the prawns with the garlic, wait until they turn pink, then pour in the peri-peri ketchup and the ketcap manis, and bring to the boil. Fold in the spring onions and serve with the rice.

Antony's tip I'm a big fan of Nando's peri-peri ketchup, but if you can't get it, just add a proprietary chilli sauce to tomato ketchup.

Serves 4

FOR THE RICE

2 tbsp vegetable oil

4 eggs, beaten with 1 tbsp soy sauce

175g (6oz) smoked streaky bacon, diced

450g (1lb) microwaveable rice

1 onion, peeled and finely chopped

150g (5oz) petits pois

4 tbsp soy sauce

1 tbsp sesame oil

White pepper

FOR THE PRAWNS

2 tbsp vegetable oil

24 large raw peeled prawns

2 cloves garlic, crushed to a paste with a little salt

250ml (9fl oz) Nando's peri-peri ketchup (whole bottle)

90ml (3fl oz) ketcap manis

4 spring onions, finely sliced

Chorizo and Leek Mash with Poached Eggs

Simply put, this neat little brunch dish is a potato nest packed full of goodies and topped with a poached egg.

Timetable: from start to table in 25 minutes
Preparation 10 minutes | Cooking 15 minutes

Put the potatoes in a large saucepan of salted water, bring to the boil and simmer until tender – about 12–15 minutes. Drain and return to the heat to dry out, then mash with the warm milk and season with white pepper.

Meanwhile, heat the olive oil in a frying pan and cook the chorizo until crispy; remove with a slotted spoon and keep warm. To the same pan, add the butter and the leeks, and cook for 5–6 minutes, until wilted. Add the sweetcorn, parsley and chorizo, and stir to combine.

At the same time, bring a pan with at least 10cm (4in) of water to the boil. Add the vinegar, then break the eggs into the rolling boil and cook for 2½ minutes. Lift out with a slotted spoon, pat dry with kitchen paper and trim any straggly white bits.

Fold the leek mixture into the mashed potato, then divide the spuds between four plates. Make an indentation in the top and spoon in the egg. Serve immediately.

Antony's tip Some prefer to break their eggs into small coffee cups before tipping them into the boiling water, claiming that this process reduces the straggly bits. That may well be, but it also creates extra washing-up! And anyway, it's easy enough to trim the eggs after cooking.

Serves 4

1kg (2¼lb) floury potatoes, peeled and cut into 2.5cm (1in) cubes

3 tbsp full-fat milk, warm

White pepper

1 tbsp good olive oil

225g (8oz) chorizo, ideally raw, cut into 1cm (½in) dice

55g (2oz) butter

2 leeks, washed and shredded

1 x 200g (7oz) can of sweetcorn, drained

2 tbsp chopped parsley

2 tbsp white wine vinegar

4 large free-range eggs

Children need a mid-morning fix, and at least with these crunch bars, you know exactly what goes into them. Isn't that better than buying a mass-produced number from the shops?

Energy-Fix Crunch Bars

Timetable: from start to table in 30 minutes | Preparation
10 minutes | Cooking 10 minutes, plus 10 minutes cooling

In a saucepan, heat the sugar, peanut butter, butter and maple syrup until melted. Fold in the fruit, nuts and Rice Krispies.

Line a square or rectangular cake tin with parchment paper, then lightly oil the surface. Spoon the mixture into the tin and smooth with a spatula or the back of a spoon. Allow to cool.

When cool, turn out onto a wire rack. Melt the chocolate in a bowl set over a pan of gently simmering water or in the microwave.

Pour the melted chocolate over the fruit slab and allow to cool. Cut into squares or rectangles, and store in an airtight container.

Antony's tip Try to buy cooking milk chocolate or dark chocolate that contains at least 55 per cent cocoa solids.

Makes 12–15

100g (3½ oz) soft
dark-brown sugar

125g (4½ oz) crunchy
peanut butter

40g (1½ oz) unsalted butter

100g (3½ oz) maple syrup

55g (2oz) dried blueberries
and cherries, roughly chopped

55g (2oz) prepared hazelnuts,
roughly chopped

100g (3½ oz) Rice Krispies

125g (4½ oz) milk or dark
chocolate

A lot of fuss is made about the health issues surrounding eating meat, but we've been doing it since we lived in caves. Like everything else in our diet, meat consumption is all about moderation. I enjoy beef about once a fortnight, and the same with lamb, so I eat red meat on average once a week.

In the UK we produce some of the best meat in the world, with excellent animal-welfare standards. Over the years I've reduced my meat consumption, and when I do buy it, I pay that little bit extra and buy the best. I buy British, and I buy local as much as possible.

I look forward to new-season lamb in spring, and I really enjoy rare-breed pork, especially the Middle White pig, which I breed. I believe that pork, more than any other meat, has to be a traditional breed; the hybrid pork that we've become used to through our supermarkets often has a cardboard texture and can be pretty tasteless. All the cuts and chops are uniform in shape with very little fat – lean, mean and a mere shadow of real pork.

My selection of meat dishes in this book covers most tastes, with an emphasis on healthy yet comforting. I've dug deep into my childhood for some of the recipes, bringing back memories of the days when we couldn't afford much with dishes such as Dumpling 'Pillows' with Bacon and Cheese. That's the food I grew up on. Nowadays, of course, we have the luxury of cheaper food and much more choice. This, however, is not always a good thing, especially since we end up missing out on the seasons.

meat

Steak always goes down well with meat-eaters, although I would limit the consumption of red meat to just once a week. You may not be a fan of anchovies, but they do turn an everyday vegetable into something truly special, so give them a try in the broccoli crush.

Pan-Fried Rib-Eye Steak with Fiery Broccoli Crush

Timetable: from start to table in under 25 minutes
Preparation 10 minutes | Cooking 12 minutes

Place the steaks in a dish. Combine the olive oil with the vinegar and garlic and paint the steaks with the marinade. Leave as long as you want – you can cook the steaks immediately if you are in a hurry.

Meanwhile, cook the broccoli in boiling salted water until tender and starting to break up – about 8 minutes. Drain well.

While the broccoli is cooking, cook the shallot and garlic in half the olive oil until soft. Add the chilli flakes and anchovies, and cook until the anchovies start to break down. Add the broccoli and roughly chop. Fold in the remaining olive oil, the capers and the Parmesan, a squeeze of lemon juice and season to taste.

To cook the steaks, drain them from the marinade and season them with salt and ground black pepper. Heat a large frying pan or griddle pan until smoking. Sear the steaks on both sides until deliciously brown, then turn down the heat and cook to your liking – 2 minutes on each side for medium-rare, 5 minutes on each side for well done. Serve with the broccoli crush, either hot or at room temperature.

Antony's tip Why not try duck, chicken breast or leg of lamb steak instead of beef.

Serves 4

FOR THE STEAKS

4 x 250g (9oz) aged rib-eye steaks

2 tbsp extra virgin olive oil

2 tbsp balsamic vinegar

2 cloves garlic, crushed to a paste with a little rock salt

FOR THE BROCCOLI CRUSH

450g (1lb) purple sprouting or tender-stemmed broccoli spears, trimmed

1 shallot, finely chopped

4 cloves garlic, finely chopped

100ml (3½ fl oz) extra virgin olive oil

½ tsp dried red chilli flakes

6 anchovies

2 tbsp baby capers, drained

4 tbsp freshly grated Parmesan cheese

Squeeze of lemon

Salt and ground black pepper

Mediterranean Steak Strips

Orange and beef may not be everyone's idea of a perfect marriage, but historically the French have always added dried orange peel to a stew. Give this a try – it contains loads of interesting flavours.

Timetable: from start to table in 20 minutes | Preparation 10 minutes, plus marinating time | Cooking 10 minutes

Put the orange zest, tarragon, Pernod and half the olive oil in a bowl, and combine with the beef strips. Allow to marinate as long as possible.

Scrape the marinade off the beef and reserve. Take the two oranges and cut between the membranes to create orange segments; put these in a bowl and squeeze the juice from the membranes and the pulp into the same bowl.

Heat the remaining oil in a frying pan until almost smoking, then cook the beef over a high heat for 1 minute. Remove, set aside and keep warm.

Add the marinade to the beef pan, along with the vinegar, spring onions, chives, anchovies, orange segments and juice, and the tomatoes. Stir to combine and bring to the boil, then add the sugar and boil until slightly sticky. Return the beef to the sauce and warm through. Serve with rice, or new potatoes and peas.

Antony's tip You can also try duck breast or chicken.

Serves 4

Grated zest of 2 oranges

1 tbsp chopped tarragon leaves

1 tbsp Pernod

4 tbsp good olive oil

450g (1lb) beef fillet or sirloin, cut into 5cm (2in) strips

2 oranges, peeled and pith removed

2 tbsp aged red wine vinegar

4 spring onions, sliced diagonally

2 tbsp snipped chives

6 anchovy fillets, finely chopped

4 plum tomatoes, deseeded and diced

2 tbsp caster sugar

Salt and ground black pepper

TO SERVE

Boiled rice or new potatoes and peas

Minted Lamb Chops on Chickpea Mash

This dish contains all the right flavours without being overpowering. It also includes a healthy mash that introduces your kids to new textures and tastes. Children may need only one chop, so reduce the quantity accordingly.

Timetable: from start to table in under 25 minutes
Preparation 10 minutes | Cooking 12 minutes

Preheat the oven to 200°C/390°F/Gas 6.

Season the lamb chops with salt and ground black pepper. Heat the tablespoon of oil in a frying or griddle pan, and cook the chops over a medium heat for 6 minutes, turning once. Remove and keep warm.

Meanwhile, use a food processor to make a mint purée. Blend the almonds, mint, parsley, garlic, lemon juice, zest and Parmesan, scraping down from time to time. Then, with the machine running, add the remaining olive oil in a thin stream. Season.

Spread a little mint purée on top of each chop, then place the chops in the oven for 8 minutes.

For the mash, heat the chicken stock in a saucepan, add the petits pois and cook for 5 minutes, then add the chickpeas and heat through. Drain but keep the stock. Mash the mixture with a potato masher, retaining some texture and adding back a little stock if it becomes too dry. Fold in the paprika and chilli sauce, then season to taste.

Place a pile of mash in the centre of each of four warm plates, then top with the chops and a scattering of mint leaves. Serve extra mint purée as required.

Antony's tip You can brown the lamb and top with the purée ahead of time, but if you are cooking the chops from cold, they will need 15–20 minutes in the oven, depending on how you like your meat cooked.

Serves 4

FOR THE LAMB

8 lamb chump chops

150ml (5fl oz) extra virgin olive oil, plus 1 tbsp extra

55g (2oz) toasted almonds

Leaves from a small bunch of mint, plus extra for garnish

4 tbsp parsley leaves

1 clove garlic, peeled

Zest of 1 organic or unwaxed lemon and juice of half a lemon

25g (1oz) freshly grated Parmesan cheese

FOR THE MASH

250ml (9fl oz) chicken stock

325g (12oz) frozen petits pois

400g (14oz) can chickpeas, drained and rinsed

1 tsp sweet paprika

1 tbsp sweet chilli sauce

Salt and ground black pepper

Lovely Mince
I call this dish 'lovely' because it turns a regular home meal into something that won't get groaned at each time you cook it.

Timetable: from start to table in 30 minutes | Preparation
15 minutes, depending on marinating time | Cooking 6 minutes

Combine together all the marinade ingredients. Add the mince and mix thoroughly, then leave for a minimum of 5 minutes or for up to 2 hours if you're organized enough.

Heat half the vegetable oil in a hot wok, then add half the mince and stir-fry for 1 minute. Remove and set aside. Repeat with the remaining oil and mince. Remove and keep warm.

Cook the Sherry or chinese cooking wine, hoisin sauce, oyster sauce and rice or cider vinegar in the wok for 1 minute. Return all the mince to the wok, add the carrot and sweetcorn, and cook over a high heat for 5 minutes. Add the spring onions and pak choi, and cook for another minute.

Spoon the lamb onto boiled rice, or serve in iceberg-lettuce leaves, and sprinkle with the sliced chillies.

Antony's tip If you're in a real hurry, buy 2-minute microwaveable rice.

Serves 4

575g (1¼ lb) lamb mince

4 tbsp vegetable oil

2 tbsp medium Sherry or Chinese cooking wine

2 tbsp hoisin sauce

2 tbsp oyster sauce

1 tbsp rice or cider vinegar

1 carrot, peeled and finely sliced

8 baby sweetcorns, halved lengthways

1 small bunch of spring onions, sliced

2 heads of pak choi, shredded

FOR THE MARINADE

2 tbsp sweet or medium Sherry

1 tbsp fish sauce

1 tbsp cornflour

5cm (2in) ginger, peeled and grated

1 tsp hot chilli sauce

2 cloves garlic, crushed to a paste

1 tsp sesame oil

TO SERVE

Boiled rice or iceburg lettuce leaves

1 red mild chilli, seeded and thinly sliced

Lamb cutlets are not the cheapest chops on offer at the butcher's, but they are tender, sweet and always well received. With this recipe you can forget the usual mint sauce or jelly, and add a little spice to your life.

Indi-Cutlets with Sweet Spiced Kachumber

Timetable: from start to table in under 25 minutes | Preparation 15 minutes, plus marinating time | Cooking 6 minutes

Combine the tandoori paste, garlic and yogurt in a bowl, add the lamb cutlets and massage gently. Leave for as long as you can. If you are short of time, a few minutes will be better than nothing.

Heat a large griddle or frying pan, add the oil and cook the cutlets according to taste – about 3 minutes each side for medium-rare.

Meanwhile, combine all the ingredients for the kachumber, then divide it between four plates and serve with the cutlets, three to a portion. Serve with rice or new potatoes.

Antony's tip Give the recipe a whirl with chicken thighs or pork chops, adjusting the cooking times accordingly, of course.

Serves 4

FOR THE CUTLETS

150g (5oz) shop-bought tandoori paste

2 cloves garlic, crushed to a paste with a little rock salt

120ml (4fl oz) Greek yogurt

12 lamb cutlets, well trimmed

1 tbsp vegetable oil

FOR THE KACHUMBER

1 small red onion, finely diced

Half a cucumber, peeled, seeded and cut into 1cm (½ in) half moons

4 plum tomatoes, seeded and roughly chopped

Juice and zest of 1 lime

1 tbsp sweet chilli sauce

1 medium-hot red chilli, finely diced

1 tbsp roughly chopped coriander

2 tsp finely chopped mint

TO SERVE

Boiled rice or new potatoes

Pork Chops with Rhubarb

When buying pork, try to buy a rare-breed variety, such as Gloucester Old Spot or Saddleback. I especially like Middle White pork: try to get your butcher to stock this breed, it is delicious. 'Pork with rhubarb?' I hear you ask. Well, why not? We eat this meat with apple, the acidity of which cuts through the richness of the pork, and rhubarb has the same acidity. Give it a go – you'll be surprised.

Timetable: from start to table in 20 minutes
Preparation 5 minutes | Cooking 15 minutes

Put the rhubarb in a saucepan and cover with water. Bring slowly to the boil, then drain immediately. Return the rhubarb to the saucepan with half the butter and the sugar, and cook gently for 10 minutes, until it has broken down to a purée.

Meanwhile, season the chops with salt and pepper. Heat the remaining butter in a frying pan until foaming, then cook the chops for 4 minutes on each side or until cooked through. Remove them and keep them warm. Tip the rhubarb into the chop pan to emulsify with the caramelized juices, scrape the bottom and mix to combine. Serve immediately with the chops, some new potatoes, carrots and a green vegetable.

Antony's tip The rhubarb goes equally well with pan-fried mackerel or herring fillets. Or, as an alternative, replace the rhubarb with gooseberries – equally tart, equally delicious!

Serves 4

6 sticks of rhubarb, cut into 2.5cm (1in) pieces

85g (3oz) unsalted butter

1 tbsp caster sugar

4 x 200g (7oz) pork chops, rind removed if you prefer

Salt and ground black pepper

TO SERVE

New potatoes, carrots and green vegetables

It's not just children who love sweet things. The moreish taste of this quick meat dish will appeal to the entire family.

Sweet and Spicy Pork

Timetable: from start to table in under 30 minutes
Preparation 15 minutes │ Cooking 12 minutes

Heat the oil in a frying pan, add the pork and cook for about 5 minutes, until browned all over. Remove from the pan and set aside.

Add the onions and red pepper to the pan, and cook for 5 minutes over a medium heat.

Meanwhile, combine the water with the sugar in a small saucepan, and heat it until the sugar has dissolved and the mixture has a deep, golden caramel colour. Add the stock – carefully, because it will spit – and stir to combine, then add the ketcap manis. Cook with the lid off until reduced by half, then add this sauce to the onion mix. Return to the heat and cook for 2 minutes.

Add the pork to the onion sauce, along with the sambal oelek, five-spice powder and spinach, and cook for 5 minutes or until the pork is cooked through. Sprinkle with spring onions and serve piping hot with boiled rice.

Antony's tip This recipe works equally well with chicken thighs, and you can add more blanched vegetables at the end of the cooking time.

Serves 4

1 tbsp non-flavoured oil

675g (1½ lb) pork fillet, trimmed and cut into 1cm (½ in) slices

1 large Spanish onion, peeled and cut into 16 wedges

1 red pepper, seeded and cut into 1cm (½ in) dice

90ml (3fl oz) water

85g (3oz) golden caster sugar

240ml (8fl oz) chicken stock

1 tbsp ketcap manis

1 tsp sambal oelek

¼ tsp five-spice powder

2 handfuls of baby spinach

TO SERVE

2 spring onions, finely sliced

Boiled rice

Pork Schnitzel Kiev

This dish gives pork, a fairly bland meat, a nice zap, loads of flavour and a crisp texture that the children will love. As many of you know, I'm a big fan of the humble anchovy in any form: fresh, in oil or salted. However, if anchovies are not for you, feel free to leave them out or replace them with some diced sun-dried tomato.

Timetable: from start to table in under 25 minutes
Preparation 15 minutes | Cooking 6–8 minutes

Wrap each pork fillet in clingfilm, place it cut side down and bash it evenly all over with a meat mallet or rolling pin until it is about 1cm (½ in) thick. Set aside.

Mash together the anchovies, garlic, parsley and butter.

With a sharp knife, cut pockets into the side of each beaten fillet and fill each with an even amount of the savoury butter. Push down the edges of the fillets to seal.

Dip the fillets into the flour on both sides, then pat off the excess. Next, dip them in the beaten eggs, followed by the breadcrumbs. Make sure each fillet is well coated.

Heat the oil in two frying pans to a depth of 0.5cm (¼in), then fry the pork for 3 minutes each side, until golden and thoroughly cooked.

Meanwhile, combine all the salad ingredients and season to taste.

Serve the pork with the salad, a wedge of lemon and a few new potatoes.

Antony's tip If you don't have two large frying pans, use one and keep the schnitzels warm in the oven while you cook the remaining fillets. A fried or poached egg on top of each schnitzel works a treat.

Serves 4

FOR THE PORK

450g (1lb) centre cut pork fillet, cut into 115g (4oz) pieces

4 anchovies in oil, drained and finely chopped

3 cloves garlic, finely chopped

2 tbsp chopped parsley

85g (3oz) unsalted butter, softened

85g (3oz) plain flour seasoned with salt, black pepper and a pinch of chilli flakes

2 free-range eggs, beaten

115g (4oz) white breadcrumbs

Olive oil for frying

FOR THE SALAD

175g (6oz) cherry tomatoes, halved

Half a red onion, finely sliced

12 basil leaves, ripped

2 tbsp extra virgin olive oil

2 tsp Sherry or balsamic vinegar

TO SERVE

Lemon wedges

New potatoes

Gammon steaks have become unpopular both at home and in restaurants, perhaps because they are perceived as too salty. However, I have tried some recently, and they have a more modern, slightly sweet taste – a taste that goes perfectly well with these delicious carrots.

Gammon Steak with Different Carrots

Timetable: from start to table in 35 minutes
Preparation 10 minutes | Cooking 25 minutes

Put the carrots in a saucepan with half the butter, the sugar and nutmeg, and just cover them with water. Place a lid over the pan and cook gently for 20 minutes. Remove the lid and increase the heat, being careful that the carrots don't stick to the bottom of the pan.

Meanwhile, in another saucepan, melt the rest of the butter over a medium heat, add the flour and cook this roux gently for 3 minutes. Slowly add the milk, stirring continuously until you have a thick sauce – about 10 minutes. Add the cream and season to taste.

Mix the sauce with the cooked carrots and stir to combine.

Meanwhile, in a large frying pan or two, heat the olive oil and cook the gammon steaks for 2–3 minutes each side, depending on their thickness, until cooked through. Serve the gammon with the carrot purée.

Antony's tip This carrot purée also goes very well with roast duck or pork. Adding a little chopped mint makes it a great partner to lamb, too.

Serves 4

450g (1lb) carrots, peeled and grated

85g (3oz) unsalted butter

1 tbsp caster sugar

1 grating of nutmeg

40g (1½ oz) plain flour

300ml (10fl oz) milk

90ml (3fl oz) double cream

Salt and ground black pepper

1 tbsp olive oil

4 x 175g (6oz) gammon steaks or bacon chops, rind snipped

Asian Surf-and-Turf Balls in Sweet-and Sour Sauce
This sophisticated yet simple Oriental combination of pork and prawns makes a perfect supper for hungry children.

Timetable: from start to table in 30 minutes
Preparation 15 minutes | Cooking 15 minutes

To make the balls, combine all the ingredients except the water chestnuts and the oil. Combine well, then take a chestnut-sized amount of the mix and roll it into a ball. Make an indentation in each ball and insert a few chopped water chestnuts in the centre; enclose them with the meat.

In a wok, pan-fry the balls in the hot oil until brown all over, then add the garlic, ginger and chilli from the sauce ingredients. Reduce the heat and cook for 5 minutes.

Add the remaining sauce ingredients except for the cornflour paste. Bring to the boil, cook for 3 minutes, then add the cornflour paste. Cook until thickened and glossy – about 2 minutes.

To serve, place some steaming rice in four warm bowls and top with the meatballs.

Antony's tip For a good, flavoursome snack, use the mix to make four large patties and serve as a burger.

Serves 4

FOR THE BALLS

325g (12oz) minced pork

325g (12oz) raw prawns, shelled and finely chopped

1 red chilli, seeded and chopped

2.5cm (1in) ginger, peeled and grated

2 spring onions, finely chopped

2 tbsp light soy sauce

2 tsp sesame oil

1 tbsp chopped coriander

1 tbsp cornflour

2 tbsp chopped water chestnuts

1 tbsp vegetable oil

FOR THE SAUCE

2 cloves garlic, finely chopped

2.5cm (1in) ginger, peeled and grated

1 chilli, deseeded and finely chopped

100ml (3½ fl oz) pineapple juice

2 tbsp light soy sauce

1 tbsp white wine vinegar

3 tbsp tomato ketchup

2 tbsp soft dark brown sugar

1 tbsp cornflour mixed with 2 tbsp cold water

TO SERVE

Boiled rice

We all love our sausages, and I happen to love beans, too, so I always enjoy this dish. It is campfire stuff, real man's food that is loved by all.

Sausage and Bean Pot

Timetable: from start to table in 35 minutes
Preparation 10 minutes | Cooking 25 minutes

Preheat the oven to 180°C/360°F/Gas 4.

In a large frying pan, heat half the olive oil and brown the sausages all over, without cooking them all the way through. Set aside and, when cool enough to handle, cut each sausage into four pieces.

In the same pan, heat the remaining oil and add the onions, garlic and bacon, and cook until the bacon is crispy and the onions are softening – about 6 minutes.

Add the Worcestershire sauce, wine, tomato sauce and the two beans, and bring to the boil. Return the sausages to the pan for a few minutes, then tip the mix into a lightly oiled baking dish.

Meanwhile, in a food processor, blend together the breadcrumbs, Parmesan, herbs and butter until green. Season with black pepper, then spoon the crumbs over the sausage mix and bake in the oven for 15 minutes, until golden. Serve with a green salad.

Antony's tip The beauty of this dish is that it can be prepared well in advance up to the crumb stage. From cold it will take 35–40 minutes in the oven to cook.

Serves 4

2 tbsp olive oil

8 favourite pork sausages

1 onion, roughly chopped

2 cloves garlic, finely chopped

4 rashers smoked streaky bacon, cut into lardons

1 tbsp Worcestershire sauce

240ml (8 fl oz) red wine

325g (12oz) favourite tomato pasta sauce

400g (14oz) can favourite baked beans

400g (14oz) can butter beans, drained and rinsed

115g (4oz) soft white breadcrumbs

25g (1oz) freshly grated Parmesan cheese

2 tbsp parsley leaves

2 tbsp snipped chives

4 sage leaves

55g (2oz) unsalted butter, melted

Ground black pepper

TO SERVE

A fresh green salad

Cheesy Sausages on Creamed Leeks and Potatoes

Occasionally, we need to live a little, try different flavours, investigate new ideas… Sausages are a British institution. This recipe is really easy and it should end up being a family favourite.

Timetable: from start to table in 35 minutes
Preparation 15 minutes | Cooking 20 minutes

Preheat the oven to 180°C/360°F/Gas 4.

Heat the oil in a frying pan, then brown the sausages all over without cooking them all the way through. Remove and set aside.

Cut a pocket lengthways in each sausage, leaving each end intact. Cut eight slivers of cheese and insert one into each pocket, then drizzle the cheese with the mango chutney.

Stretch the rashers of bacon with the back of a knife, then wrap one around each sausage to encase the cheese and mango chutney.

Place the sausages, cut side up, back in the frying pan, making sure it's oven-proof (if not, place them on a shallow roasting tray). Cook in the oven for 10–12 minutes, until the sausages are cooked, the bacon is crispy and the cheese bursting to get out.

Meanwhile, cook the potatoes in boiling salted water for 8–10 minutes, until tender, then drain. Cook the leeks in the butter in a saucepan or frying pan with the thyme for 8–10 minutes, until softened. Add the cooked potatoes and the cream, and cook for another 5 minutes, until thickened. Season to taste.

Serve the sausages on a bed of creamed leeks and potatoes.

Antony's tip By all means, use your favourite sausages – my personal preference is pork and leek. You can also use savoy or pointed cabbage instead of leeks, finely shredded and cooked the same way.

Serves 4

FOR THE SAUSAGES

1 tbsp olive oil

8 pork sausages

225g (8oz) Stinking Bishop, Waterloo or Brie cheese

2 tbsp smooth mango chutney

8 rashers of dry-cured bacon

FOR THE LEEKS AND POTATOES

450g (1lb) new potatoes, quartered lengthways

450g (1lb) leeks, washed and shredded

55g (2oz) unsalted butter

1 tsp soft thyme leaves

150ml (5fl oz) double cream

Salt and ground black pepper

Dumpling 'Pillows' with Bacon and Cheese

Nowadays, it is common to waste up to 30 per cent of the food we buy. But in days gone by, families were usually more thrifty. I remember this dish very well – it is very substantial but costs little to make.

Timetable: from start to table in 30 minutes
Preparation 10 minutes | Cooking 20 minutes

Place a deep saucepan of salted water on to boil.

Meanwhile, beat the flour with the eggs until thick and smooth, then gradually add the milk, beating the mixture until it no longer clings to a wooden spoon. Fold in the chives and season with salt and pepper. Set aside and allow to rest.

While the dumpling batter is resting, heat a large frying pan and cook the bacon for 3–4 minutes, until starting to crisp, then add the butter and onions, and cook until the onions are golden – about 10 minutes.

Scoop up a dessertspoon of the dumpling batter. Dip the spoon into the boiling salted water, knocking the handle sharply on the side of the saucepan, so the mix drops into the water. Repeat with the rest of the mixture as quickly as you can. Make sure that you release the dough gently from the bottom of the saucepan to stop it sticking. The dumplings will float to the surface. Cook them for 8 minutes, then, with a slotted spoon, scoop them up and place them lightly in the bottom of a buttered baking dish.

Toss the dumplings gently with the onion mix, then sprinkle over the Gruyère cheese. Bake under a hot grill until the bubbling and golden.

Antony's tip Try mixing the dumplings with peas, bacon and cheese, roasted peppers or tomato sauce and cheese. The possibilities are endless, including mixing grated Parmesan into the dumpling batter.

Serves 4

450g (1lb) plain flour

2 free-range eggs

300ml (10fl oz) milk

2 tbsp snipped chives

Salt and ground white pepper

175g (6oz) smoked streaky bacon, cut into lardons

25g (1oz) unsalted butter, plus a little extra for greasing

2 large onions, finely chopped

115g (4oz) Gruyère cheese, grated

This is a wonderfully comforting dish based on an Irish dish called pan haggerty but with a few AWT add-ons. It takes about 45 minutes, but it is worth the wait.

Schnuggies in a Skillet

Timetable: from start to table in 45 minutes
Preparation 15 minutes | Cooking 30 minutes

Combine the onions, cheeses, meats, herbs, garlic, nutmeg and seasonings. Set aside.

Place a heavy 23cm (9in) frying pan or shallow casserole over a medium heat and add the oil and clarified butter.

Layer half the potatoes over the base of the pan, season and top with the onion-and-cheese mix. Cover with the remaining potatoes, pour in the chicken stock and dot the top with softened butter. Cover with foil and cook on the hob for 15 minutes.

Remove the foil and cook for a further 15 minutes. Place the frying pan under a hot grill to colour the top potato layer.

Antony's tip Semi-frozen bacon is easier to dice than refrigerated bacon. If you don't fancy chorizo, use your favourite pork sausages, but be sure to brown them first, before cutting them into 2.5cm (1in) chunks.

Serves 6

450g (1lb) onions, grated

85g (3oz) Cheddar cheese, grated

85g (3oz) cows' mozzarella, grated

115g (4oz) streaky bacon, cut into strips

115g (4oz) chorizo sausage, sliced and cut into strips

1 tbsp mixed fennel seeds, rosemary and thyme leaves

2 cloves garlic, finely chopped

A pinch of nutmeg

Salt and ground black pepper

2 tbsp olive oil

2 tbsp clarified butter

675g (1½ lb) potatoes, peeled, parboiled, and thinly sliced

150ml (5fl oz) chicken stock

25g (1oz) butter

Hot Spaghetti with Three Beans, Pancetta and Parmesan This fresh, summery pasta dish requires little cooking and excites the palate with its seasonal flavours.

Timetable: from start to table in 20 minutes
Preparation 5 minutes | Cooking 15 minutes

Place the cannellini beans in a food processor with the garlic, basil and half the olive oil. Blend to a purée, season with salt and black pepper, and set aside.

Meanwhile, bring a large deep pot of salted water to the boil and cook the spaghetti for a couple of minutes less than the manufacturer's directions – about 8–9 minutes for dried pasta. For the last 4 minutes of cooking, add the two types of green beans. Drain the pasta and immediately combine it with the cannellini-bean purée.

Meanwhile, whisk together the mustard, lemon juice and half the remaining olive oil. At the same time, fry the pancetta in the remaining olive oil. Pour the dressing and the pancetta onto the pasta, and toss to combine.

Divide the pasta between four bowls and sprinkle with the Parmesan cheese.

Antony's tip Pasta cools quickly, so always heat the serving plates or bowls before you dish it up.

Serves 4

400g (14oz) can cannellini beans, drained and rinsed

2 cloves garlic

12 basil leaves

100ml (3½ fl oz) extra virgin olive oil

Salt and ground black pepper

450g (1lb) spaghetti

225g (8oz) podded or frozen broad beans

175g (6oz) fresh extra fine French beans, cut into 2.5cm (1in) pieces

2 tsp Dijon mustard

Juice of half a lemon

115g (4oz) pancetta, diced

TO SERVE

55g (2oz) freshly grated Parmesan cheese

If you struggle to get your children to eat a variety of vegetables, you might want to ply them with this twist on a classic Italian pasta dish. They will love it!

Five-a-Day Spaghetti Carbonara

Timetable: from start to table in 25 minutes
Preparation 10 minutes | Cooking 15 minutes

Bring a large saucepan of deep water to the boil and add a teaspoon of salt. Grab the spaghetti in one fistful, twist it so it fans out and place vertically into the deep water. As it softens, the spaghetti will collapse into the water. Stir for a couple of minutes to stop the pasta sticking together.

Meanwhile, heat the oil and butter in a frying pan until foaming, add the pancetta or bacon, and cook until crispy – about 5 minutes. Add the onions, garlic and mushrooms, reduce the heat and cook gently for 7–10 minutes, until the onions are soft but not coloured.

Meanwhile, beat all the eggs in a bowl big enough to take the spaghetti, then fold in the grated Parmesan cheese and a few grindings of black pepper.

Four minutes before the pasta has finished cooking, add the broccoli and peas to the boiling water. When the pasta is cooked, drain it in a large colander and immediately add it to the beaten eggs and cheese, stirring to combine. Fold in the spinach and allow the heat of the pasta to wilt it, then add the bacon-and-mushroom mix and the tomatoes. Season to taste and serve immediately.

Antony's tip To keep the spaghetti al dente, cook for a couple of minutes less than it says in the manufacturer's directions.

Serves 4

400g (14oz) dried spaghetti

30ml (1fl oz) good olive oil

25g (1oz) unsalted butter

115g (4oz) pancetta or smoked streaky bacon, cut into 1cm (½in) lardons

1 small onion, finely diced

1 clove garlic, crushed to a paste with a little rock salt

85g (3oz) button mushrooms, sliced

2 whole free-range eggs plus 2 egg yolks

55g (2oz) freshly grated Parmesan

16 small broccoli florets

115g (4oz) frozen petits pois

2 handfuls of spinach

2 tomatoes, seeded and diced

Salt and ground black pepper

A Spring Pasta with Garlic Cream This cream
pasta dish takes no time to prepare and satisfies most taste buds. If you're
a vegetarian, simply leave out the bacon.

Timetable: from start to table in 20 minutes
Preparation 10 minutes | Cooking 10 minutes

For the topping, heat one tablespoon of the olive oil in a frying pan.
Cook the bacon until crispy, then add the onions and cook until
golden. Add the leeks and thyme, and cook for 2 minutes. Heat the
remaining oil in a separate frying pan, add the rosemary, garlic and
breadcrumbs, and cook until the crumbs are golden brown and crispy,
constantly turning them over. Fold in the lemon zest and the crispy
bacon mixture.

Meanwhile, in a saucepan, melt the cream cheese in the double cream;
when this mixture is smooth, add the peas and spinach leaves, and
cook for 3 minutes. Fold in the tomatoes and season to taste.

At the same time, bring a deep pot of salted water to the boil. Cook
the pasta in boiling water until al dente – about 3 minutes for fresh
pasta. Drain, then add to the sauce. Spoon the pasta into four warm
bowls and scatter with the bacon crumbs.

Antony's tip Ignore that old wives' tale of putting oil in the
water when cooking pasta. It's a waste of money, since the oil just
floats to the surface.

Serves 4

FOR THE PASTA

115g (4oz) garlic cream cheese
(such as Boursin)

150ml (5fl oz) double cream

115g (4oz) frozen petits pois

1 handful of baby spinach
leaves

2 tomatoes, seeded and diced

450g (1lb) fresh penne

Salt and ground black pepper

FOR THE TOPPING

6 tbsp extra virgin olive oil

175g (6oz) rindless back
bacon, cut into lardons

1 onion, finely chopped

2 leeks, washed and shredded

½ tsp chopped thyme

1 tsp finely chopped rosemary

1 tsp finely chopped garlic

85g (3oz) white breadcrumbs

Grated zest of 1 unwaxed
lemon

poultry

Poultry is an excellent source of protein. However, if you're buying chicken, it's important to choose carefully. If you have read the reports and seen the TV programmes, then you are probably aware how cheap chicken is reared. I buy only organic chicken. I believe in the organic movement – not only for the taste, but because I try to keep chemicals out of my body. But then, I can afford to eat organic produce, and I am aware that not everyone can. If you can't, I urge you to buy free-range chicken, which will only add a small cost to every portion. It's not the best, but it is better than barn-reared.

However, my message shouldn't be all doom and gloom. Good chicken is delicious and much lower in saturated fats than most meats, so it should feature regularly as part of your diet. In this chapter I offer you 12 of my favourite quick chicken dishes, plus a token duck offering. When it comes to cooking chicken, people often worry about any bacteria that may be present. Consequently, just like turkey, chicken tends to be overcooked. If you're concerned, buy a meat thermometer: if the internal temperature reaches 72–75°C (161–167°F) for at least five minutes, you can be confident that your chicken is safe and it's still going to be juicy; if it reaches 90°C (194°F), it will be safe but also very dry.

Enjoy your chicken, buy the best you can afford and don't overcook it.

This granny-style recipe hails from an era when nothing was ever wasted. It's deliciously moreish, and the mash is perfect winter fodder.

Marmalade Chicken with a Mash of Roots

Timetable: from start to table in 30 minutes
Preparation 10 minutes | Cooking 20 minutes

Preheat the oven to 180°C/360°F/Gas 4.

For the chicken, combine all the ingredients except the thighs and oil in a bowl, then put the chicken into the mixture and massage the flesh. Heat the oil in an ovenproof frying pan and place the thighs in the pan with the marinade. Place in the oven for 20 minutes, or until cooked through, turning the chicken and basting every 5 minutes.

Meanwhile, cook the carrots and potatoes in boiling salted water for 5 minutes, then add the parsnips and cook for a further 10 minutes, or until the vegetables are tender. Drain well and mash with the butter. (You're looking for some texture here, so be sure not to make the mash too smooth.) Season with white pepper and perhaps a little salt.

Divide the mash between four warm plates, top each with two pieces of chicken and sprinkle with spring onions, if using.

Antony's tip If you prefer to leave the skin on the thighs, brown the chicken in the pan before cooking it in the oven.

Serves 4

FOR THE CHICKEN

4 tbsp of your favourite marmalade

5cm (2in) ginger, peeled and grated

3 cloves garlic, crushed to a paste with a little salt

2 tsp Dijon mustard

60ml (2fl oz) fresh orange juice

8 chicken thighs, skinless, flesh slashed

1 tsp olive oil

FOR THE MASH

4 carrots, peeled and sliced

2 floury potatoes, peeled and cut into 2.5cm (1in) dice

4 medium parsnips, peeled and sliced

55g (2oz) unsalted butter

Ground white pepper and salt

TO SERVE

3 spring onions, thinly sliced (optional)

Crispy Spiced Chicken with Interesting Spinach

Spinach For some reason, chicken thighs are not popular with the British public. I've been campaigning for people to use them more because they are deliciously sweet and succulent and also great value for money.

Timetable: from start to table in 40 minutes
Preparation 10 minutes | Cooking 30 minutes

Preheat the oven to 180°C/360°F/Gas 4.

Combine the spices with the harissa, salt and honey in a bowl; add the chicken thighs and massage the mixture into the flesh and skin. Heat the oil in a frying pan and cook the thighs skin side down for 10 minutes on a low to medium heat, placing a piece of parchment paper over them and topping with another pan to weigh them down. Then place the chicken thighs in the oven. After 10 minutes remove the paper and continue to cook the chicken for a further 10 minutes, making sure the skin doesn't get anything more than golden. Do not move or turn over the chicken. When the chicken is cooked through and the juices run clear when pierced, remove from the oven and keep warm.

Meanwhile, heat the oil in a wok or large saucepan. Cook the garlic and onions over a medium heat for 5 minutes, add the chilli flakes, spinach, sultanas and pine nuts, and cook until the spinach has wilted. Season with lemon juice, salt and pepper, then put the spinach in a sieve to squeeze out most of the excess liquid. Serve under the chicken with a dollop of yogurt.

Antony's tip In an ideal world, you would buy whole peppercorns and cumin and coriander seeds, toast them lightly in a dry frying pan until the aromas are released, then crush them using a pestle and mortar or an electric coffee grinder.

Serves 4

FOR THE CHICKEN

1 tsp ground coriander

1 tsp ground cumin

1 tsp ground black pepper

1 tbsp harissa

1 tsp sea salt

1 tsp clear honey

8 chicken thighs, skin on but boneless, if possible

1 tbsp good olive oil

FOR THE SPINACH

5 tbsp extra virgin olive oil

3 cloves garlic, crushed to a paste with a little salt

1 onion, finely chopped

A pinch of dried chilli flakes

1kg (2 ¼lb) spinach, stalks removed, well washed

4 tbsp sultanas

2 tbsp toasted pine nuts

Squeeze of lemon juice

Salt and ground black pepper

TO SERVE

Greek yogurt

Crunchy Nut Chicken, White Beans and Chorizo

The name of this recipe reflects a family joke, since my son's preferred breakfast cereal is Crunchy Nut cornflakes, which has nothing to do with this recipe! This dish does, however, have nuts and is a firm favourite.

Timetable: from start to table in under 35 minutes
Preparation 15 minutes | Cooking 18 minutes

Preheat the oven to 180°C/360°F/Gas 4.

For the chicken, blitz the nuts, seeds, spices and biscuits in a food processor, retaining a little texture. In a bowl, combine the hummus with the harissa. Make shallow slashes in the top of the chicken breasts, then spread a thin coating of hummus over the top and pat in the nut crumbs. Drizzle each chicken breast with a little olive oil.

Heat the remaining olive oil in a frying pan and cook the chicken, uncoated side down, over a medium heat for 3 minutes. Then, place the chicken in the oven for 15–18 minutes or until cooked through (this will depend on the size of the breasts.)

Meanwhile, for the beans, heat the oil in a frying pan. Add the chorizo and cook for 2–3 minutes, turning once until crispy. Remove the chorizo and set aside, leaving behind the red oils.

Cook the onion and garlic for 5 minutes until softened, then add the beans and roasted peppers, and cook for 2 minutes to warm through. Finally, add the remaining ingredients, returning the chorizo to the mix. Toss to combine and season to taste.

Place a pile of beans in the centre of four warm bowls, then top with the chicken breasts.

Antony's tip You can also try the crunchy-nut topping on lamb or pork chops. If chorizo is not to your taste, replace it with pancetta or smoked streaky bacon.

Serves 4

FOR THE CHICKEN

40g (1½ oz) pine nuts

40g (1½ oz) almonds

15g (½ oz) sesame seeds

1 tsp toasted coriander seeds

1 tsp toasted cumin seeds

3 digestive biscuits

2 tbsp shop-bought hummus

1 tsp harissa

4 chicken breasts, skinless

2 tbsp olive oil

FOR THE WHITE BEANS

4 tbsp extra virgin olive oil

175g (6oz) chorizo, sliced, preferably raw

1 onion, finely chopped

2 cloves garlic, finely chopped

1 x 400g (14oz) can cannellini beans, drained and rinsed

3 roasted peppers, from a shop-bought jar, chopped

Juice and zest of 1 unwaxed lemon

2 tbsp flat-leaf parsley leaves

Salt and ground black pepper

Retro Chicken with Mushrooms and Bacon

Golden oldies, or recipes from times gone by, often make great, moreish dishes. This recipe combines many of the flavours that we all love.

Timetable: from start to table in under 30 minutes
Preparation 8 minutes | Cooking 20 minutes

Preheat the oven to 180°C/360°F/Gas 4.

Wrap each chicken breast in a slice of Parma ham; if necessary, secure the two together with a cocktail stick.

Heat half the butter in a large frying pan and cook the chicken breasts for 3 minutes, until the Parma ham is crispy all over. Move the chicken from the frying pan to a flat roasting tray and pop it in the oven for 12 minutes or until cooked through.

While the chicken is in the oven, add the bacon lardons to the frying pan and cook until crisp – about 4 minutes – then add the onions and mushrooms, and cook over a medium heat for 6 minutes, until the onions have softened.

Pour the chicken stock into the frying pan and reduce the liquid by half over a fierce heat, then add the white wine and, again, reduce by half.

Add the peas and cook for 2 minutes; beat the double cream with the flour and pour into the frying pan, letting it cook for 5 minutes until it has thickened. Season to taste.

Remove the chicken from the oven to four warm plates, pour the sauce over and serve with new potatoes or mash.

Antony's tip Remember to cook your new potatoes while the chicken is cooking, so that everything is ready at the same time.

Serves 4

4 free-range chicken breasts

4 slices of Parma ham

55g (2oz) unsalted butter

115g (4oz) smoked bacon lardons

1 onion, finely chopped

115g (4oz) button mushrooms, halved

75ml (2½fl oz) chicken stock

75ml (2½fl oz) white wine

115g (4oz) frozen petits pois

150ml (5fl oz) double cream

1 tsp plain flour

TO SERVE

New potatoes or creamy mash

If you want to impress with a bright and colourful dish, you can do it the easy way by buying antipasti vegetables in oil. These shop-bought jars are a brilliant standby.

Mediterranean Chicken Skewers

Timetable: from start to table in 30 minutes
Preparation 10 minutes │ Cooking 20 minutes

Soak eight long wooden skewers in cold water at the same time as the mushrooms.

Meanwhile, combine the olive oil with the lemon juice, zest and honey. Season with salt and pepper, and toss the chicken into the mixture. Marinate for 10 minutes.

Thread all the ingredients onto the skewers, making sure you have a bay leaf next to each piece of chicken – so, bay leaf, chicken, grilled vegetable, mushroom and so on – until the skewers are full.

Cook the skewers on a barbecue or a lightly oiled frying pan or griddle pan for 5 minutes each side, until browned all over and thoroughly cooked. Baste with the marinade from time to time.

Serve with rice and salad.

Antony's tip Select your grilled vegetables according to your tastes. Courgettes and aubergines are great alternatives. Soaking the mushrooms stops them going dry and leathery when on the grill. If you have time, leave the chicken to marinate for longer.

Serves 4

16 button mushrooms, soaked in cold water for 5 minutes

3 tbsp extra virgin olive oil

Juice and grated zest of 1 unwaxed lemon

2 tsp clear honey

Salt and ground black pepper

2 large skinless chicken breasts, about 500g (1lb 2oz) in total, each cut into equal sized pieces

1 jar each roasted red peppers, roasted artichokes and roasted baby onions

16–24 bay leaves

From time to time we have to make supper in a flash using store-cupboard ingredients. Next time you find yourself in this situation, try making this dish.

Red-Pepper Gnocchi with Chicken

Timetable: from start to table in 20 minutes
Preparation 10 minutes | Cooking 10 minutes

Serves 4

450g (1lb) or 1 packet fresh shop-bought gnocchi

115g (4oz) frozen petits pois

1 tbsp extra virgin olive oil

2 cloves garlic, crushed to a paste with a little salt

½ tsp chilli flakes

Half a jar roasted red peppers, roughly chopped

1 packet shop-bought béchamel sauce

3 tbsp double cream (optional)

2 tbsp red pepper pesto

2 cooked chicken breasts, cut into 2.5cm (1in) pieces

55g (2oz) freshly grated Parmesan cheese

Heat a saucepan of salted water until it is boiling, then add the gnocchi and the peas. Cook until the gnocchi dumplings float to the top – about 5 minutes – and drain.

Meanwhile, heat the oil in a frying pan, add the garlic and chilli flakes and cook gently for 2 minutes. Add the roasted peppers, béchamel sauce, cream (if using) and red-pepper pesto, and bring to the boil. Then add the gnocchi, peas and chicken, and warm through – about 3–4 minutes. Place into warmed bowls, top with grated Parmesan and serve immediately.

Antony's tip To create an excellent vegetarian version of this dish, leave out the chicken and add extra green vegetables when cooking the gnocchi. For the more mature palate, try substituting black-olive paste for the red-pepper pesto.

On a trip to New Orleans, I was given the opportunity to discover the secret of Tabasco sauce, which was first produced in 1868. What a great set-up: a rare piece of foodie culture in a country where food history tends to be a little limited. What impressed me most was the purity of the sauce – no heat treatment, just the original recipe.

Spicy Chicken Wings with Blue-Cheese Dip

Timetable: from start to table in 25 minutes
Preparation 10 minutes │ Cooking 15 minutes

To make the blue-cheese dip, blend together the soured cream, mayonnaise, vinegar, spring onions, garlic, cheese and Tabasco sauce in a food processor until smooth. Season to taste and set aside.

Heat 5cm (2in) of vegetable oil in a large saucepan to 180°C/360°F. Fry the chicken wings until golden and crispy – about 12–15 minutes. Drain on kitchen paper and keep warm.

Mix together the butter, ketchup and Tabasco sauce. Toss the hot cooked wings into this mixture and dust with cayenne pepper and salt.

Serve the chicken wings hot with the blue-cheese dip.

Antony's tip You may need to fry the chicken in batches, in which case keep the cooked wings warm in the oven.

Serves 4

Vegetable oil for frying

12 chicken wings, halved, wing tips discarded

85g (3oz) unsalted butter, melted

2 tbsp tomato ketchup

1 tsp Tabasco sauce

Cayenne pepper

FOR THE BLUE-CHEESE DIP

150ml (5fl oz) soured cream

150ml (5fl oz) mayonnaise

2 tsp white-wine vinegar

2 tbsp sliced spring onions

1 clove garlic, finely diced

85g (3oz) blue cheese, crumbled

1 tsp Tabasco sauce

Salt and ground black pepper

Chilli Lime Chicken with a Broccoli Stir-Fry

This recipe is a great way to add interest to your greens. Simply zap up the chicken and then serve to hungry children. No objections, no arguments – they will just love it.

Timetable: from start to table in 30 minutes
Preparation 10 minutes | Cooking 20 minutes

Preheat the oven to 180°C/360°F/Gas 4.

Combine the sweet chilli sauce, two tablespoons of soy sauce and the lime juice. Pour over the chicken thighs and leave as long as possible – if you're in a hurry, 5 minutes is better than nothing.

Place the thighs skin side down in an ovenproof, oiled frying pan and cook for 3 minutes, painting the thighs with the marinade on a regular basis. Turn the thighs over and place them in the oven to cook for 12–15 minutes or until cooked through.

Meanwhile, heat one tablespoon of the oil in a large wok, and fry the onion and the black beans (if using) until golden brown over a high heat – about 5 minutes.

Combine the remaining soy sauce, rice vinegar, Chinese cooking wine or sherry and remaining oil, and tip into the onion-and-black-bean mixture.

Add the broccoli to the onions and cook for 3 minutes, stirring regularly. Finally, add the oyster sauce and heat through. Divide the vegetables between four warm plates and top with sticky chicken.

Antony's tip The same marinade can also be used with excellent results on pork chops.

Serves 4

90ml (3fl oz) sweet chilli sauce

3 tbsp soy sauce

2 tbsp fresh lime juice

8 chicken thighs
(thigh fillets, if possible)

2 tbsp vegetable oil
(plus extra for oiling)

1 large onion, roughly chopped

1 tbsp salted dried black beans, rinsed and mashed (optional)

1 tbsp rice vinegar

1 tbsp Chinese cooking wine or dry Sherry

450g (1lb) small broccoli florets

2 tbsp oyster sauce

How do you make a dull bit of chicken jump off the plate and zap your taste buds? Try this. It's different, and your little people will be screaming for more.

Yummy Chicken with Coconut Mash

Timetable: from start to table in 35 minutes | Preparation and marinating at least 20 minutes | Cooking 15 minutes

For the chicken, first make a coriander paste by blending together all the ingredients except the chicken in a mini food processor. Carefully lift the skin off the chicken breast without separating it completely from the flesh, creating a pocket. Spoon some of the coriander paste under the skin, rub it in well and reshape the skin. Leave to marinate for at least 10 minutes (maximum overnight).

Heat the remaining one tablespoon of sunflower oil in a heavy-based frying pan, then cook the chicken breasts, skin side down, over a medium heat for 10 minutes. Turn them over and cook on the flesh side for 5 minutes or until cooked through.

While the chicken is cooking, combine all the ingredients for the mash except the spinach, season to taste and heat (in a non-stick frying pan, if possible) over a low flame or in the microwave until piping hot. Fold in the spinach and continue to cook until it has wilted.

Place a pile of mash in the centre of four plates, then top with the spicy chicken breast.

Antony's tip I'm a bit of a leg man, so I often make this dish with chicken thighs – again, pushing the coriander paste under the skin.

Serves 4

FOR THE CHICKEN

2.5cm (1in) ginger, peeled and grated

2 cloves garlic, peeled and crushed

2 tbsp sweet chilli sauce

1 tsp hot chilli sauce

3 tbsp coriander leaves

1 tbsp mint leaves

2 tsp sesame oil

1 tbsp sunflower oil, plus 1 extra for cooking

4 chicken breasts, skin on

FOR THE MASH

675g (1½ lb) home-made or shop-bought mash

150ml (5fl oz) coconut cream

2 hot red chillies, finely chopped

1 tbsp Thai green curry paste

2 tsp fish sauce (nam pla)

2 tsp clear honey

Salt and ground black pepper

2 handfuls of baby spinach leaves, washed

Fishcakes, chicken, burgers… I love 'em all to bits, so I decided to put them together in this dish. It's a double whammy!

Thai-Influenced Chicken and Prawn Burgers with a Sweet Dipping Sauce

Timetable: from start to table in 20 minutes
Preparation 10 minutes | Cooking 10 minutes

Start by preparing the dipping sauce. Combine all the ingredients and allow the flavours to develop for as long as possible.

Next, prepare the burgers. In a food processor blend together the chicken, garlic and curry paste until smooth, then scrape the mixture into a bowl. Add the remaining ingredients except the oil and season with a little salt.

Using wet hands, shape the mixture into eight medium-sized patties. Heat the oil in a large frying pan and cook the burgers for 3 minutes each side, until golden and cooked through. You may have to cook the burgers in batches, so keep them warm until they are ready to serve. Serve with a crunchy salad (see page 138).

Antony's tip These burgers can be made ahead as raw patties and stored overnight in the fridge, where they will firm up.

Serves 4

FOR THE BURGERS

2 chicken breasts, skinless and roughly chopped

1 clove garlic, crushed

2 tbsp Thai red curry paste

250g (9oz) raw jumbo prawns, shelled and chopped

55g (2oz) fresh breadcrumbs

200g (7oz) can sweetcorn

4 spring onions, fully chopped

2 tbsp chopped coriander

1 red chilli, seeded and finely chopped

Pinch of salt

1 tbsp vegetable oil

FOR THE DIPPING SAUCE

4 tbsp sweet chilli sauce

4 tbsp lime juice

1 tbsp soy sauce

1 tbsp chopped coriander

1 tsp chopped mint

1 tsp grated ginger

2 spring onions, finely chopped

Chicken and Lemongrass Lettuce Wraps

This recipe has lots of different ingredients, but if your store cupboard and fridge are well stocked, you'll have no problem. Plus, it's really easy to prepare. Anything the children can wrap, they will, and you'll be happy in the knowledge that it's fast food but not junk food.

Timetable: from start to table in under 25 minutes
Preparation 10 minutes | Cooking 12 minutes

Heat the oil in a wok, add the lemongrass, chillies, ginger and garlic, and stir-fry quickly for 1 minute. Add the chicken mince, breaking it up into small granules. Cook for 5 minutes, stirring constantly.

Add the curry paste and stir to combine, then add the mangetout, carrots, fish sauce and honey, and stir-fry for 5 minutes. Finally, fold in the spring onions, coriander and lime juice. Serve immediately, wrapped in the lettuce leaves. Remember the napkins!

Antony's tip If chicken is not for you, this dish also works well with pork mince. Sprinkle the final mixture with a few chopped peanuts for that authentic Oriental vibe.

Serves 4

1 tbsp peanut or vegetable oil

2 stalks lemongrass, outside leaves removed and very finely chopped

2 small red Thai chillies (hot), finely chopped

2.5cm (1in) ginger, peeled and grated

3 cloves garlic, crushed to a paste with a little salt

450g (1lb) chicken mince

1 tbsp Thai red curry paste

85g (3oz) mangetout, finely shredded

1 carrot, peeled and diced

2 tbsp fish sauce (nam pla)

1 tbsp clear honey

4 spring onions, cut thinly on the diagonal

Half a bunch of coriander, roughly chopped

Juice of 1 lime

Iceberg lettuce leaves

I love one-pot food: it saves on the washing-up and wins family hearts. Packed full of flavour, this chicken dish always goes down a treat.

Chicken in an Asian Pot

Timetable: from start to table in 35 minutes
Preparation 15 minutes | Cooking 20 minutes

Heat the oil in a large saucepan and fry the curry paste for 2 minutes, until it releases its fragrance. Add the lemongrass, ginger, garlic, lime leaves, chillies and turmeric, and cook for a further 2 minutes.

Pour in the coconut milk, chicken stock and carrots, and bring to the boil, before simmering for 8 minutes.

Meanwhile, remove the chicken meat from the carcass and shred with two forks, discarding the bones. Add the meat to the broth and heat through for 5 minutes, then fold in the fish sauce, lime juice, coriander and spring onions.

Serve in warmed bowls, topped with the coriander leaves, bean sprouts and chopped peanuts (if using).

Antony's tip Other green vegetables (broccoli, sugar snaps, baby spinach, asparagus etc) can be added with the spring onions for a more substantial stew.

Serves 4

1 tbsp non-flavoured oil

1 tbsp Thai green curry paste

1 tbsp finely chopped lemongrass

1 tsp grated ginger

2 cloves garlic, crushed to a paste with a little salt

3 lime leaves, shredded

2 small hot green chillies, finely sliced

½ tsp ground turmeric

2 x 300g (11oz) cans coconut milk

400ml (14fl oz) chicken stock

2 carrots, peeled and finely sliced

1 small rotisserie-cooked chicken

1 tbsp fish sauce (nam pla)

Juice of 2 limes

Handful of coriander leaves and soft stalks

3 spring onions, finely sliced

TO SERVE

12 coriander leaves, chopped

Handful of bean sprouts, soaked in iced water

2 tbsp chopped unsalted roasted peanuts (optional)

Soy-Glazed Duck with Asian Greens This dish was inspired by the lovely Jo Pratt, who is a regular on my Cooks shows on ITV. Healthy and fun at the same time – and that's just Jo!

Timetable: from start to table in 25 minutes
Preparation 10 minutes | Cooking 15 minutes

Place the duck breasts, skin side down, in a dry non-stick frying pan and cook for 8–10 minutes, discarding (or saving for another purpose) the fats that come out of the duck. Turn the duck over and cook for another minute. Allow to cool slightly.

In a wok, cook the juice and zest from the oranges, add the garlic, ginger, chilli, soy sauce, sugar and sesame oil, and continue to cook until it starts to thicken – about 3 minutes. Slice the duck, then toss it in the sauce to glaze.

Remove the duck, leaving the juices, and add two tablespoons of water to the wok, then add the pak choi, asparagus and sugar snaps, and cook for 3 minutes. Return the duck to the wok to warm through, then divide it between four warm bowls, scattering with spring onions and sesame seeds.

Antony's tip It is easy to adapt this recipe to all sorts of protein: tofu, halloumi, chicken or pork.

Serves 4

2 duck breasts, skin slashed

Juice and zest of 2 organic oranges

2 cloves garlic, crushed to a paste with a little rock salt

2.5cm (1in) peeled ginger, grated

A pinch of dried chilli flakes

2 tbsp dark soy sauce

2 tbsp soft dark brown sugar

2 tsp sesame oil

2 pak choi, roughly chopped

8 asparagus tips, cut into 2.5cm (1in) pieces

55g (2oz) sugar snaps, topped and tailed

TO SERVE

4 spring onions, finely sliced

1 tbsp sesame seeds

Why don't we eat more fish? Here in Britain, we are surrounded by water, yet on average we eat less than one portion of fish a week. It's a depressing fact that could easily be remedied.

We should aim to eat two portions of fish each week, one of which should be an oily fish such as mackerel, sardines or herring, which are rich sources of omega-3 fatty acids and are healthy for the heart. As a chef, whenever I see a fillet of fish, I see supper on the table in 10 minutes – fish is the healthiest fast food we have.

There are so many exciting ways of cooking and preparing fish, and it doesn't have to be cod, either. In fact cod, along with many other British favourites, is best avoided unless we want to drive it to extinction. This means that, for sustainability, we need to eat varieties such as pollack, dab, gurnard and the humble trout, which represents amazing value for money.

In this chapter I've offered you 16 tasty, easy fish dishes that I hope will excite your taste buds. Some are classics, while some have an up-to-date slant. There are plenty of fishy offerings in the 'Soups, Salads & Snacks' chapter, too.

fish

I love fish, but many people seem somewhat nervous about cooking it at home. This is a shame, because fish is the healthiest fast food you can get. This recipe is a great opportunity to use sustainable fish such as pollack or whiting; failing that, it works perfectly well with any white fish fillets.

Fish in Sauce

Timetable: from start to table in 30 minutes
Preparation 10 minutes │ Cooking 20 minutes

Scatter the base of a buttered baking dish with half the shallots, half the mushrooms, the thyme and the bay leaf. Lay the fish fillets on top, and season with salt and white pepper. Place the remaining shallots and mushrooms and all the peas on top of the fish. Pour in the wine, cover with foil and cook for 10 minutes over a medium heat.

Remove the foil, then drain the wine carefully into a saucepan and reduce the liquid by half over a high heat. Meanwhile, keep the fish warm. Beat the flour into the cream and pour onto the reduced wine, cooking gently for 5 minutes. Season to taste. Pour the sauce over the fish and serve immediately.

Antony's tip If you want to be really retro, pipe a ring of mashed potato around the fish while the sauce is cooking. Pour the sauce into the centre, then scatter with Gruyère cheese and flash the lot under the grill.

Serves 4

3 shallots, finely chopped

85g (3oz) button mushrooms, thinly sliced

1 sprig of thyme

1 bay leaf

4 x 175g (6oz) fillets of whiting or pollack, skinless

Salt and ground white pepper

85g (3oz) frozen petits pois

375ml (13fl oz) dry white wine

½ tsp plain flour

150ml (5fl oz) double cream

One of the finest simple suppers is a bowl of spaghetti flavoured with extra virgin olive oil, chilli, garlic and parsley. So I thought to myself, 'Why not add some nuggets of fish?' Same cooking time, but no more effort – and lots more health.

Fish in a Flash

Timetable: from start to table in 25 minutes
Preparation 10 minutes | Cooking 15 minutes

Cook the spaghetti in deep boiling salted water for 2 minutes less than the manufacturer's directions. Drain and drizzle with one tablespoon of the olive oil.

Meanwhile, heat the remaining olive oil in a frying pan, add the garlic and both chillies, and cook gently for 3–4 minutes to infuse the flavour. Add the Martini, fish stock and butter, and boil vigorously until emulsified.

Next, add the fish and watercress, and cook for 2 minutes. Fold in the parsley and season to taste.

Tip the fish mixture onto the spaghetti and toss to combine. Serve immediately.

Antony's tip The alcohol will disappear during the cooking process. However, if you're concerned about it, feel free to omit the Martini. This dish is also great with prawns or chicken.

Serves 4

375g (13oz) dried spaghetti

4 tbsp extra virgin olive oil

3 cloves garlic, crushed to a paste with a little salt

2 whole medium-hot red chillies

2 tbsp dry Martini

200ml (7fl oz) fish stock

55g (2oz) unsalted butter

450g (1lb) white fish fillets (eg halibut, sea bass), skinless and cut into 1cm (½ in) pieces

1 bunch of watercress with short stems

2 tbsp finely chopped parsley

Ground black pepper and lemon juice, to taste

Smoked Haddock with Cheesy Potato

Potatoes are among my favourite vegetables. They can be cooked in
a hundred different ways, but very few of us ever think of using them
to make a sauce. This is an excellent supper dish.

Timetable: from start to table in 25 minutes
Preparation 10 minutes | Cooking 15 minutes

Heat the milk in a saucepan with the onions and bay leaf. When it
starts to simmer, add the fish and cook for 4 minutes. Remove the
fish and set aside, then strain the cooking liquid.

Meanwhile, cook the garlic and thyme in half the butter for 1 minute.
Add the potatoes and 450ml (15fl oz) of the cooking liquid, and
cook until the potatoes are tender – about 8 minutes.

Flake the smoked haddock and fold it into the potato mix. Fold in the
spring onions, Parmesan and remaining butter. Season to taste.

Warm through the poached eggs and place one on each of four
warm plates. Top with the smoked-haddock and potato mix and
serve with some rocket leaves and black pepper.

Antony's tip If you prefer the dish a little less rich, poach the
fish in stock and use that instead of milk to cook the potatoes.

Serves 4

600ml (1 pint) milk

2 onions, halved

1 bay leaf

675g (1½ lb) undyed smoked
haddock

1 clove garlic, finely chopped

1 sprig of thyme

50g (2oz) unsalted butter

4 medium potatoes, peeled
and cut into 5mm (¼in) dice

4 spring onions, finely sliced

100g (3½oz) freshly grated
Parmesan

Salt and ground black pepper

4 poached eggs, precooked
(see page 30)

TO SERVE
A handful of rocket leaves

Sea bass with crispy skin is a real pleasure, and it goes particularly well with greens flavoured with bacon and cheese.

Crispy-Skinned Sea Bass on Bacon Greens

Timetable: from start to table in 20 minutes
Preparation 10 minutes | Cooking 10 minutes

Season the sea bass fillets with salt and ground white pepper, then dip the skin side only in the seasoned flour. Heat the oil in a large non-stick frying pan and cook the fillets, skin side down, over a medium heat for 6 minutes. The fish will try to curl up as soon as it hits the heat, so push it down with a fish slice so that the whole surface of the skin remains in contact with the heat.

Add the butter to the pan, then turn the fish over onto its flesh side, basting it with the butter. Turn off the heat and allow the fish to finish cooking gently from the heat of the pan.

Meanwhile, for the greens, cook the bacon in hot oil in a frying pan until golden. Add the butter, then the leeks and cabbage, and cook for 3–4 minutes, until wilted. Increase the heat and add the cream. Cook until thickened – about 2 minutes – then fold in the Parmesan and season to taste.

Spoon the greens in the centre of each of four warmed plates and top with the sea bass and some of the fish juices. Serve with some crusty bread.

Antony's tip If you are not keen on cabbage and leeks, try frying some onions with the bacon and adding diced courgettes; then follow the recipe in the normal way.

Serves 4

FOR THE SEA BASS

4 x 175g (6oz) sea bass fillets, skin on, scaled

Salt and ground white pepper

Seasoned flour

1 tbsp olive oil

25g (1oz) unsalted butter

FOR THE BACON GREENS

6 rashers of streaky bacon, cut into lardons

1 tbsp olive oil

25g (1oz) unsalted butter

3 leeks, cut into thin slices

A quarter savoy cabbage, cored and very finely shredded

150ml (5fl oz) double cream

25g (1oz) freshly grated Parmesan cheese

TO SERVE

Slices of fresh, crusty bread

Spaghettini with Halibut, Breadcrumbs and Parsley Simplicity is the best route when I am in the mood for purity of flavours. And this dish certainly delivers.

Timetable: from start to table in 20 minutes
Preparation 5 minutes | Cooking 15 minutes

Cook the pasta in plenty of boiling salted water, until al dente – about 5–7 minutes.

Meanwhile, heat the olive oil in a frying pan, add the garlic, chilli flakes and anchovy fillets, and cook, stirring regularly, until the anchovies have disintegrated.

Add the breadcrumbs and fry until golden. Remove and set aside. Add the fish to the same pan and fry over a high heat, turning the pieces over gently, for about 5 minutes or until the fish is just cooked.

Drain the pasta and toss with the fish. Season with salt and pepper.

Mix in the parsley, drizzle with the extra virgin olive oil and lemon juice, and fold in the anchovy breadcrumbs.

Antony's tip Halibut can be replaced with any other white fish. If you really want to treat yourself, try using turbot.

Serves 2

325g (12oz) dried spaghettini

2 tbsp olive oil

1 clove garlic, finely chopped

1 pinch of dried chilli flakes

4 anchovy fillets, chopped

55g (2oz) fresh breadcrumbs

275g (10oz) halibut fillet, cut into 2.5cm (1in) cubes

Salt and ground black pepper

A small bunch of chopped flat-leaf parsley leaves

1 tbsp extra virgin olive oil

2 tsp lemon juice

Basil-Crumbed Mackerel, Roast Tomatoes and Red Pepper Sauce

Mackerel is a full-flavoured fish that is woefully underused, even though it can easily be included in our diet as one of the oily fish that we should eat at least once a week. Here, I've given it a lovely crunch.

Timetable: from start to table in 20 minutes
Preparation 10 minutes │ Cooking 10 minutes

Preheat the oven to 200°C/390°F/Gas 6.

In a food processor, blend together the basil, Parmesan, breadcrumbs and two tablespoons of olive oil. Scoop out, season and place in a bowl. Wash out the blender, dry it, then blend all the sauce ingredients. Season and set aside.

Sprinkle the skin side of the mackerel with the Cajun seasoning. Paint the flesh side with the beaten egg yolk, then spread it with the herb breadcrumbs.

Place the fish onto an oiled baking tray, breadcrumb side up. Scatter over the tomatoes and season well. Drizzle the tomatoes and fish with the remaining olive oil.

Bake for 8–10 minutes until the crumbs are golden, the fish flakes easily when pressed with a knife and the tomatoes are soft.

Serve with the red pepper sauce and a small rocket salad.

Antony's tip The red pepper sauce makes a great topping for other fish, pork and poultry dishes, too.

Serves 4

FOR THE FISH

Leaves from 1 bunch of basil

25g (1oz) freshly grated Parmesan

85g (3oz) fresh breadcrumbs

5 tbsp extra virgin olive oil

4 large mackerel fillets

1 tsp shop-bought Cajun seasoning

Yolk of 1 free-range egg

200g (7oz) cherry tomatoes, halved

FOR THE SAUCE

4 roasted red peppers from a shop-bought jar

1 tbsp sweet chilli sauce

1 tsp hot chilli sauce

2 tbsp powdered almonds

2 tbsp extra virgin olive oil

Juice of half a lemon

Salt and ground black pepper

TO SERVE

Rocket salad

Herring is a versatile, sustainable fish, full of the right fats and exceptionally good value. And that's without mentioning its delicious taste! Despite all this, not many people include herring in their diet. Give this simple recipe a go and you'll soon be eating it on a regular basis.

Herring Crumb Bake

Timetable: from start to table in 15 minutes
Preparation 5 minutes | Cooking 10 minutes

Preheat the oven to 200°C/390°F/Gas 6.

Mix the mustard with the sugar, vinegar, salt and pepper, and spread over the herring fillets.

Arrange the fillets in a greased ovenproof dish. Sprinkle with the breadcrumbs and drizzle with the oil or melted butter. Bake in the oven for 10 minutes, until golden and bubbling. Serve with salad and new potatoes.

Antony's tip When you get your fishmonger to fillet the herrings, ask him or her to remove any pin bones (that's the small, annoying bones), otherwise you will face a long and painful job with the tweezers at home.

Serves 4

85g (3oz) English mustard
1 tbsp golden caster sugar
1 tbsp white wine vinegar
Salt and pepper
8 fresh herring fillets
55g (2oz) white breadcrumbs
2 tbsp oil or melted butter

TO SERVE
Fresh green salad
New pototoes

Roast Fish Fillets with Coconut, Coriander and Lime

It's time to get a little more adventurous with your fish dishes! The good news is that healthy doesn't have to mean boring: the calories for this delicious dish amount to just over 300 per person.

Timetable: from start to table in under 25 minutes | Preparation 10 minutes, plus marinating time | Cooking 12 minutes

Throw the first six ingredients into a food processor and blend to a fine paste. Add half the oil and pulse to combine.

Combine this paste with the coconut.

Slash one side of each fish fillet three times. Spread the mixture over the slashed sides and marinate while heating the oven to 200°C/390°F/Gas 6.

Lightly grease a flat roasting tray with the remaining oil. Arrange the fish fillets, coriander side up, on it and place in the hot oven. Cook for 12 minutes. Serve with steamed baby pak choi and plain rice.

Antony's tip To extract coconut flesh easily, place the coconut in a hot oven for 10 minutes. This will loosen the flesh from the shell. Then tap around the circumference with the back of a heavy knife or hammer. Do this over a bowl, so as to catch the juices when you break open the coconut. If you can't be bothered (but do try – it makes so much difference!), simply soak some desiccated coconut in cold water for 10 minutes, then squeeze-dry before using.

Serves 4

1 bunch of coriander (stalks and all), roughly chopped

2 hot chillies, seeded

2 cloves garlic, peeled and halved

2.5cm (1in) piece of ginger, peeled and cut into four

Juice and zest of 1 lime

2 tsp clear honey

2 tbsp non-flavoured oil

55g (2oz) freshly grated coconut or soaked desiccated coconut (see tip)

4 x 175g (6oz) fillets of cod, haddock or salmon

TO SERVE

Steamed baby pak choi

Boiled rice

You're in a hurry, as usual. If you happen to have some organic farmed salmon in the fridge and a well-stocked store cupboard, this recipe's for you: light, quick and not a bit fiddly. And if you use two-minute microwaveable rice, you'll be sitting around the dinner table in no time!

Pan-Fried Salmon with Eastern Influences

Timetable: from start to table in 20 minutes
Preparation 10 minutes | Cooking 10 minutes

Dust the salmon skin with the seasoned flour. Heat the oil in a large frying pan, place the salmon, skin side down, in the pan and cook over a medium heat for 8 minutes, until the skin is crispy and the salmon flesh is three-quarters cooked. Turn the salmon over and cook it on the flesh side for 2 minutes, then remove and set aside to keep warm.

In the same pan, add the butter, soy sauce, garlic, ginger, chilli and honey, and whisk to combine. Add the pak choi and cook over a high heat for 2 minutes. With a slotted spoon, lift out the pak choi onto four warm plates, then top with the salmon. Quickly add the lime zest and juice to the juices in the pan, and spoon over the salmon. Serve with plain rice.

Antony's tip Adding a few chopped coriander leaves to the pak choi makes this dish even more delicious. However, be aware that not all children like coriander.

Serves 4

4 salmon fillets, skin on

3 tbsp seasoned plain flour

1 tbsp vegetable oil

85g (3oz) unsalted butter

3 tbsp soy sauce

2 cloves garlic, crushed to a paste

2.5cm (1in) ginger, peeled and grated

1 red chilli (medium hot), finely chopped

1 tbsp clear honey

4 heads of pak choi, sliced lengthways

Juice and grated zest of 2 limes

TO SERVE

Boiled rice

Teriyaki Salmon with Courgette Chips

Sticky salmon is lovely – the sweetness of the sauce combined with the flavour of the salmon really works. And who doesn't love courgette chips?

Timetable: from start to table in 20 minutes
Preparation 10 minutes | Cooking 10 minutes

For the courgettes, put 5cm (2in) of vegetable oil in a wok and heat it up.

For the salmon, heat the vegetable oil in a frying pan and cook the fish, skin side down, until the skin is crispy – about 6 minutes. Turn over and cook for 2 minutes on the flesh side. Remove and keep warm.

To the salmon pan, add the soy sauce, sugar, sesame oil and garlic, and cook over a medium heat until sticky. Return the salmon to the pan and glaze all over with the sticky soy.

Meanwhile, combine the cayenne pepper with the seasoned flour. Dip the courgette matchsticks in the milk, then into the flour and shake off the excess. Cook in the hot oil for 2 minutes, then drain on kitchen paper and serve with the salmon.

Antony's tip This recipe works well with most fish fillets, especially yellowfin tuna.

Serves 4

FOR THE SALMON

1 tbsp vegetable oil

4 x 175g (6oz) salmon fillets, skin on

8 tbsp soy sauce

4 tbsp soft dark brown sugar

1 tbsp sesame oil

3 cloves garlic, crushed to a paste

FOR THE COURGETTE CHIPS

Vegetable oil for frying

1 tsp cayenne pepper

200g (7oz) seasoned plain flour

2 courgettes, cut into matchsticks

210ml (7fl oz) milk

You are just back from work and now need to feed the family…
Time may be short, but there is no need to resort to ready meals
and takeaways. This is a quick dish, and tasty too.

Retro Salmon Supper

Timetable: from start to table in under 25 minutes | Preparation
5 minutes | Cooking, including mash, under 20 minutes

Melt the butter in a pan, stir in the flour and cook for a few minutes
without colouring. Gradually stir in the milk and cook until the sauce
is thick. Bring to boiling point and add the lemon juice.

Fold in the flaked salmon and the prawns, heat through and season
to taste with salt and pepper.

Pipe a deep border of hot mashed potatoes around the edge of a
gratin dish. Spoon the fish mixture into the centre and sprinkle with
chopped parsley. Serve with buttered peas.

Antony's tip You can speed things up even more by folding
the salmon and prawns into a tub of ready-made béchamel sauce. If
you're not into piping potatoes, just serve the fish in its sauce,
alongside the mash.

Serves 4

40g (1½ oz) unsalted butter

40g (1½ oz) plain flour

600ml (1 pint) milk

1 tbsp lemon juice

420g (15oz) canned salmon,
drained and flaked

250g (9oz) peeled cooked
prawns (defrosted if frozen)

Salt and pepper

325g (12oz) hot mashed
potatoes

TO SERVE

Chopped parsley

Buttered peas

My children love stir-fries; in fact, they love most things with an Oriental slant. And so do I – they're quick to prepare and quick to cook!

Prawn and Green Vegetable Stir-Fry

Timetable: from start to table in 25 minutes
Preparation 15 minutes | Cooking 10 minutes

Heat half the oil in a hot wok, then add the ginger, garlic and onions, and cook over a high heat for 2 minutes. Add the asparagus and broccoli, and stir-fry continuously for 2 minutes, then add the sugar snaps and cook for 1 minute. Remove the vegetables and keep warm.

Add the remaining oil to the wok and cook the prawns over a high heat until pink – about 3 minutes. Return the vegetables to the wok, then add the remaining ingredients and cook until heated through, about 2 minutes. Serve with rice.

Antony's tip Add some precooked egg noodles to the wok for a more substantial stir-fry.

Serves 4

1 tbsp groundnut or vegetable oil

5cm (2in) ginger, peeled and grated

2 cloves garlic, crushed to a paste with a little salt

1 onion, roughly cut

115g (4oz) asparagus, cut into 2.5cm (1in) pieces

2 stalks of broccoli, peeled and thinly sliced

115g (4oz) sugar snaps, topped and tailed

24 large uncooked king prawns, shelled and deveined

1 red chilli (medium hot), finely sliced

2 tbsp rice wine or dry Sherry

60ml (2fl oz) soy sauce

½ tbsp sweet chilli sauce

TO SERVE

Boiled rice

A Simple Prawn Curry Keep this curry simple and mild, and you've got a child-friendly dish that adults will lap up as well.

Timetable: from start to table in under 25 minutes
Preparation 8 minutes | Cooking 15 minutes

In a bowl, combine the prawns with the lemon juice and zest, a quarter of the garlic, the salt and half the turmeric. Massage the prawns and leave for 10 minutes.

In the meantime, heat half the oil in a wok or large frying pan, add the remaining garlic, the ginger and onions, and cook for 5 minutes. Add the spices, including the remaining turmeric, and the green pepper, and fry for 2 minutes. Add the tomatoes, bring to the boil and cook for 5 minutes.

Heat the remaining oil in another frying pan. Drain the prawns from their lemon bath, pat them dry and fry them over a medium heat for 2 minutes, or until they turn pink. Once done, tip them into the curry, add the lime juice and coriander, and stir to combine. Cook for 1 minute. Serve with basmati rice.

Antony's tip Don't be tempted to use cooked prawns! You really need the flavours to permeate the prawns. Plus, let's face it, they hardly take any time to cook anyway.

Serves 4

500g (1lb 2oz) raw jumbo prawns, peeled

Juice and grated zest of 1 unwaxed lemon

4 cloves garlic, crushed to a paste with a little salt

1 tsp salt

1 tsp turmeric

3 tbsp vegetable oil

5cm (2in) ginger, peeled and grated

1 onion, roughly chopped

½ tsp ground chilli powder

1 tsp ground coriander

1 tsp ground cumin

1 tsp garam masala

1 green pepper, cut into small dice

400g (14oz) can chopped tomatoes

Juice of 1 lime

Half a bunch of coriander, roughly chopped

TO SERVE

Boiled basmatic rice

There's always room in a child's culinary range for good old classics. This is one of the best spaghetti dishes, made popular in the 1960s and 1970s in every Italian restaurant. Small baby clams weren't always available in the UK at that time, so more often than not, they would use canned clams, which is exactly what I'm going to do with this recipe.

Spaghetti Vongole

Timetable: from start to table in 25 minutes
Preparation 10 minutes | Cooking 15 minutes

Drain the clams, retaining their juices. Place the juices in a saucepan, bring to the boil and cook until the liquid has reduced by half, then set aside. Put a large pan of deep salted water on to boil, ready for the spaghetti.

Meanwhile, in another saucepan, heat the oil, then add the onions and garlic, and cook over a medium heat until the onions are starting to soften – about 5 minutes. Add the oregano or marjoram, anchovies, chilli flakes and tomatoes, along with the reduced clam juices, and cook until the sauce is quite thick. Check for seasoning: because of the clam juices, the sauce shouldn't need any salt, but it might need black pepper. Fold in the clams and parsley, and keep warm.

Meanwhile, cook the pasta for a couple of minutes less than the manufacturer's directions, drain and tip into the sauce. Stir to combine, then spoon onto four warm plates.

Antony's tip If you are using fresh clams or mussels, cook them in a glassful of boiling dry white wine until they open. Save the juices and take up the recipe from Step 2. You'll need 1.5kg (3lb) of fresh shellfish for this recipe.

Serves 4

290g (11oz) can clams in the shell

290g (11oz) can shelled clams

60ml (2fl oz) good olive oil

1 onion, finely chopped

4 cloves garlic, finely chopped

2 tsp fresh oregano or marjoram, chopped

3 anchovies, chopped

½ tsp dried chilli flakes

400g (14oz) can chopped tomatoes

Ground black pepper

2 tbsp chopped parsley

450g (1lb) spaghetti

Asian Steamed Mussels

Many people seem to be nervous about mussels; this is unfortunate, because mussels are packed full of flavour and they represent remarkable value. This recipe uses classic French principles and zaps them with an Asian kick.

Timetable: from start to table in 25 minutes
Preparation 10 minutes | Cooking 15 minutes

Combine the cooking wine or mirin, soy sauce or tamari, lime juice and zest, honey and black-bean sauce, and heat in a small saucepan, simmering for 5 minutes.

Meanwhile, in a wok or large saucepan, heat the oil with the ginger, garlic and chillies, and cook for 3 minutes. Add the cooked wine mixture to the wok (be careful: it will splutter) and return to the boil. Add the mussels and shake to combine. Cover the pan with a lid and cook over a fierce heat for 5 minutes, shaking from time to time.

Add the coriander leaves and spring onions, and toss to combine. Serve immediately, discarding any mussels that have not opened.

Antony's tip No luck in purchasing cooking wine or mirin? Then substitute them with dry Sherry or some Sauvignon Blanc from Australia or New Zealand.

Serves 4

150ml (5fl oz) Chinese cooking wine or mirin

1 tbsp soy sauce or tamari

Juice and zest of 1 lime

2 tsp clear honey

1 tbsp black-bean sauce

1 tbsp non-flavoured oil

1 tsp grated ginger

2 cloves garlic, crushed to a paste

2 red hot chillies, seeded and finely sliced

2kg (4½ lb) fresh mussels, cleaned

A handful of coriander leaves

2 spring onions, finely sliced

This dish offers a lovely combination of Mediterranean flavours that adds a little something to run-of-the-mill squid.

Mediterranean Squid and Vegetable Casserole

Timetable: from start to table in 30 minutes
Preparation 15 minutes | Cooking 15 minutes

Cook the onions in half the olive oil with the garlic, anchovies and chilli, until the onions are soft but not brown.

Add the aubergine and cook for 5 minutes, stirring regularly.

Add the oregano or marjoram, basil and courgettes, and cook until the courgettes start to wilt – about 3 minutes.

Finally, add the roasted red peppers, tomatoes and vinegar. Heat through.

Meanwhile, towards the end of the vegetable cooking time, pan-fry the squid in the remaining olive oil over a high heat for about 1 minute. Take care not to overcook the squid, since it will then become very tough.

Just before serving, add the squid to the vegetables. Season to taste and garnish with basil leaves.

Antony's tip The vegetable mix makes a good base for other forms of protein, too. Try it with chicken, prawns or fillets of fish.

Serves 6

2 onions, peeled and roughly chopped

4 tbsp extra virgin olive oil

2 cloves garlic, peeled and chopped

2 anchovies, mashed

1 chilli, finely chopped

1 aubergine, peeled and cut into 2.5cm (1in) cubes

2 tbsp oregano or marjoram leaves

2 tbsp ripped basil leaves

225g (8oz) courgettes, thinly sliced

4 roasted red peppers, from a shop-bought jar, sliced

200g (7oz) can chopped tomatoes

1 tbsp balsamic vinegar

450g (1lb) squid, cleaned and cut into small squares

Salt and ground black pepper

TO SERVE

A handful of fresh basil leaves

veggies

I never serve vegetarian food that tries to replicate the look, smell or taste of meat. I don't do nut rissoles, and I hate vegetarian bacon, sausages and Quorn. When nature provides so many wonderful vegetables and man has created pasta, why get excited by meat replicas? When I want to cook vegetarian food, which I often do, my culinary mind wanders down to the Mediterranean, over to North Africa, across to the Middle East, and into India, Pakistan and the Far East, where a bounty of vegetarian dishes exists.

As well as the dishes in this chapter, you'll find many recipes in other chapters that can easily be adapted by the omission of the meat or fish element. When cooking vegetables, you need to cook them fast in order to retain their nutrients. Steaming is my method of choice, but recent studies tell us that microwaving is also excellent.

As a chef, I tend to use a deep pan full of boiling, lightly salted water. It's important that the water is deep, so that it returns to the boil quickly and the cooking is almost instant. If you are cooking vegetables for a lot of people, plan ahead by having a large bowl of iced water at the ready, so that you can blanch your veggies for a short time and then spoon them into the cold water; this sets the colour and arrests the cooking process, and it can be done several hours ahead of serving. When needed, the vegetables can be reheated in boiling salted water or tossed in olive oil or butter.

Tomato and Cheese Stack

As your children get older, their taste buds develop (hopefully), and you can lead them down a more sophisticated path. This is a great recipe to start with.

Timetable: from start to table in 25 minutes
Preparation 10 minutes | Cooking 15 minutes

Preheat the oven to 200°C/390°F/Gas 6.

Arrange the tomato slices in a shallow ovenproof dish, so that they overlap slightly. Drizzle with the vinegar and season. Tuck the slices of cheese between the tomatoes, then tear the basil leaves over the top.

Tear the bread into small pieces and mix with the oil and garlic. Sprinkle the bread over the tomatoes, then place in the oven for 15 minutes until the cheese has melted and the breadcrumbs are crisp and golden. Serve with a green salad.

Antony's tip Try this stack with a combination of Mediterranean vegetables, such as courgettes or fried aubergines. How about a little black-olive paste between each layer?

Serves 4

4 beefsteak tomatoes, sliced horizontally

4 tsp balsamic vinegar

Salt and ground black pepper

115g (4oz) cows' mozzarella, drained and thinly sliced

A small bunch of fresh basil

85g (3oz) ciabatta bread

2 tbsp extra virgin olive oil

2 cloves garlic, finely chopped

TO SERVE

A crisp green salad

Cheese and Onion Wedges Please, don't go all 'holier than thou' on me! Children deserve a plate of fun from time to time, as do adults, and these potato wedges taste great.

Timetable: from start to table in 40 minutes
Preparation 10 minutes │ Cooking 30 minutes

Preheat the oven to 200°C/390°F/Gas 6.

Place the potato wedges on a lightly oiled flat roasting tray and season with salt and pepper. Place in the oven and cook according to the manufacturer's directions – approximately 25 minutes.

Meanwhile, heat a frying pan. Combine the garlic, onion and chillies, and place the mix in the pan with the butter. Cook until the onion is soft – about 8–10 minutes.

Tip the wedges into an ovenproof dish, scatter with the onion mix and the grated cheese, and return to the oven for a further 5 minutes or until the cheese has melted.

Just before serving, drizzle with the sweet chilli sauce.

Antony's tip Non-vegetarians may enjoy frying some pieces of bacon with the onions.

Serves 4

675g (1½ lb) frozen potato wedges

Non-flavoured oil for greasing

Salt and ground black pepper

2 cloves garlic, crushed to a paste with a little sea salt

1 large onion, peeled and finely diced

2 green chillies, finely chopped

25g (1oz) unsalted butter

85g (3oz) grated Cheddar or Emmental cheese

2 tbsp sweet chilli sauce

A Cheesy Fondue
I can't think of another dish that has been so derided over the years, but the truth is that everyone loves a fondue – they just don't like admitting it! So dig out that wedding present and introduce your children to a tasty blast from the past.

Timetable: from start to table in 25 minutes
Preparation 5 minutes | Cooking up to 20 minutes

Prepare the table: get your burner set up, croutons ready, chilled white wine for the grown-ups, forks for dipping and plenty of paper napkins.

Rub your fondue pot with the cut clove of garlic, then put it over a medium heat. Add the cheese, wine and pepper, then, as the wine boils, get beating.

If the cheese clubs together in a mass and won't join forces with the wine, use the flour, mixing it with a little cold wine to a thin, milky consistency. Add this little by little, whisking continuously. Gradually, the harmonization of the ingredients will take place, and the mixture will thicken. At this point, add the Kirsch but keep beating for about 10 minutes to remove the strong alcohol taste.

Season with nutmeg and more pepper if required.

Antony's tip I know it's traditional to serve croutons with your fondue, but you can also have any of the following at the ready: cooked new potatoes, asparagus, broccoli, cauliflower, cooked sausages and crunchy apple.

Serves 4

1 clove garlic

400g (14oz) Gruyère, Emmental or Raclette cheese, cut into very small dice

300ml (10fl oz) dry white wine

Ground white pepper

½ tsp potato flour or plain flour

90ml (3fl oz) Kirsch

A pinch of nutmeg

TO SERVE

Two-day-old 2.5cm (1in) bread croutons

If you can't be bothered to make the real thing, these Oriental egg 'pancakes' are just the ticket. Quick and great value, they're perfect if you're in a hurry.

Thai-Inspired Vegetable 'Pancake'

Timetable: from start to table in under 30 minutes
Preparation 15 minutes | Cooking 12 minutes

Heat the oil in a large frying pan, add the curry paste and fry over a medium heat for 1 minute. Add the garlic, onion, carrot and red pepper, and cook for 5 minutes, then add the sweetcorn, peas, tomatoes and cabbage, and cook for 3 minutes. Fold in the honey, fish sauce, pepper, coriander and mint, and stir to combine. Set aside and keep warm.

Meanwhile, in a bowl, beat together the eggs and fish sauce until you obtain a very thin mixture. Heat a little oil in a non-stick frying pan to cover the base. Pour in a little egg mixture and tip the pan, as you would for pancakes, to coat its entire surface. Cook for 30 seconds until the egg is dry. Tip out onto a work surface and repeat three more times.

Spoon some vegetable filling into the centre of the egg pancakes and fold in the sides to create a parcel. Repeat, keeping warm in a low oven. Serve immediately.

Antony's tip These egg pancakes can be made ahead, then placed on a flat roasting tray, covered with foil and reheated in a 180°C/360°F/Gas 4 oven for 10 minutes when required.

Serves 4

FOR THE FILLING

2 tbsp vegetable oil

1 tbsp Thai red curry paste

2 cloves garlic, finely chopped

1 large onion, finely chopped

1 carrot, peeled and diced

1 red pepper, seeded and diced

1 small can sweetcorn, drained

85g (3oz) frozen petits pois

2 tomatoes, seeded and diced

¼ savoy cabbage, finely shredded

1 tsp clear honey

2 tbsp fish sauce (nam pla)

½ tsp black pepper

1 tbsp chopped coriander

1 tsp chopped mint

FOR THE EGG PANCAKES

5 eggs

1 tbsp fish sauce (nam pla)

Vegetable oil for frying

There are times when I just fancy a bowl of noodles or fried rice – no protein, just energy-giving carbs. However, I also need flavour, and that's where this dish delivers. I would normally use fish sauce and oyster sauce, but since I've gone all vegetarian for this section, I've replaced them with soy sauce and black-bean sauce.

Pad Thai Vegetarian Noodles

Timetable: from start to table in 15 minutes
Preparation 10 minutes | Cooking 5 minutes

Soak the rice noodles in a bowl of boiling water, according to the manufacturer's directions, until soft. Drain.

Put a wok over a high heat and add the oil. When the oil starts to smoke, add the shallots, spring onions, chillies and garlic paste, and stir-fry for 1 minute.

Add the noodles to the wok, then the soy sauce, Chinese wine or sherry, lime juice, honey and black-bean sauce. Stir-fry for 3 minutes, combining well. Fold in the coriander and the nuts (if using), tip into a large warm bowl and serve immediately.

Antony's tip This recipe is good for using up leftover vegetables or even prawns or precooked chicken or pork.

Serves 2

225g (8oz) flat dried rice noodles

2 tbsp vegetable oil

3 shallots, finely chopped

3 spring onions, finely sliced diagonally

3 red medium-hot chillies, seeded and thinly sliced

3 tbsp garlic paste

3 tbsp soy sauce

1 tbsp Chinese cooking wine or dry Sherry

Juice of 1 lime

2 tbsp clear honey

2 tbsp black bean sauce

3 tbsp chopped coriander

1 tbsp chopped peanuts (optional)

Oh, Sugar – I've Got Nothing in for Supper

We've all been there, and probably more times than we care to recall. When that happens, that is what store cupboards are for: big-time cheating! Just don't tell the children…

Timetable: from start to table in 15 minutes
Preparation 5 minutes │ Cooking 10 minutes

Fill a large saucepan with cold, heavily salted water and bring to the boil.

Heat the butter in a large saucepan, add the mushrooms and toss to coat. Add two tablespoons of water, cover with a lid and cook for 3 minutes. Add the mushroom soup and heat through.

Cook the pasta for a couple of minutes less than the manufacturer's directions to keep it al dente. Then, with a pasta ladle or tongs, lift the pasta and drop it into the mushroom sauce. Toss to combine and check the seasoning.

Spoon the pasta into a large warm bowl and sprinkle with Parmesan. Serve immediately with a leafy salad.

Antony's tip Try a variety of soups – chicken, tomato or asparagus will all work well – or, dare I say it, a bottled pasta sauce, some of which are pretty good.

Serves 4

55g (2oz) unsalted butter
175g (6oz) button mushrooms, quartered
1 can condensed mushroom soup
325g (12oz) dried fettuccine or linguine
Salt and ground black pepper

TO SERVE

55g (2oz) grated Parmesan cheese
A leafy salad

Fresh Fettuccine Tricolore

For a hot bowl of something, you can't get much faster than this pasta dish full of simple ingredients. It is best made when tomatoes have lots of flavour, which in the UK means late summer or early autumn.

Timetable: from start to table in under 20 minutes
Preparation 8–10 minutes | Cooking 8 minutes

Put a large saucepan of heavily salted water on to boil.

Toast the coriander seeds in a dry pan until you can smell their aroma, then remove and crush them with a mortar and pestle or the base of a clean saucepan. Place the seeds in a large saucepan with the garlic, chillies and oil. Heat to no more than 65°C (150°F), or hand hot, infuse for 5 minutes, then add the tomatoes, lemon juice and half the basil. Season with salt and plenty of ground black pepper. Warm through until the basil changes colour.

Meanwhile, cook the fettuccine according to the manufacturer's directions – usually, if fresh, 2–3 minutes. Lift the pasta, with dripping water, with a pasta ladle and place it into the tomato oil. Toss to combine. Divide the pasta between four warm bowls, grate the feta or push it through a fine sieve to create a snow effect over the pasta, and dot with the remaining basil leaves.

Antony's tip If you wish, you could add black olives, red peppers or artichokes to this dish.

Serves 2

2 tsp coriander seeds

2 cloves garlic, crushed to a paste with a little salt

2 dried hot chillies

6 tbsp extra virgin olive oil

8 ripe plum tomatoes, seeded and roughly chopped

Juice of 1 lemon

16 basil leaves, ripped

Salt and ground black pepper

450g (1lb) fresh fettuccine

TO SERVE

55g (2oz) feta cheese

This dish is always popular with the oldies, who remember eating it as children, so why not pass the secret of macaroni cheese on to the next generation so they can enjoy it, too?

Very Cheesy Macaroni Cheese

Timetable: from start to table in 30 minutes
Preparation 5 minutes | Cooking 25 minutes

Preheat the oven to 200°C/390°F/Gas 6.

Cook the pasta in deep boiling salted water for 3 minutes less than the manufacturer's directions, drain and return to the saucepan.

Immediately add the butter and toss to coat. Then add the ricotta, blue cheese, half the Emmental, the double cream and mustard. Stir until the cheese has melted and everything is well combined, then season with pepper.

Tip the pasta into a lightly oiled baking dish. Combine the remaining Emmental with the Parmesan, and scatter this cheesy mix over the pasta. Place in the oven and cook for 10–12 minutes, until bubbling and golden. Serve with a leafy salad.

Antony's tip This can be made in advance and refrigerated. From cold, it will take 25–30 minutes in a hot oven.

Serves 4

400g (14oz) dried macaroni or penne

25g (1oz) unsalted butter

200g (7oz) ricotta cheese

85g (3oz) blue cheese, ideally gorgonzola or dolcelatte

115g (4oz) grated Emmental cheese cheese

150ml (5fl oz) double cream

2 tsp English mustard

Ground white pepper

25g (1oz) freshly grated Parmesan cheese

TO SERVE

A leafy salad

Something Nice to Do with Tofu

Tofu certainly has its uses, but boy, do you need to bang in a load of flavour to bring it to life! I love its texture but I want more out of it. This recipe delivers on the flavour stakes.

Timetable: from start to table in 25 minutes
Preparation 10 minutes | Cooking 15 minutes

Dry the tofu as much as possible. Heat four tablespoons of the oil in a large non-stick frying pan and cook the tofu gently over a medium heat until golden all over. Drain on kitchen paper and set aside.

Meanwhile, in another frying pan, heat the remaining oil. Add the onions, garlic, chilli and ginger, and stir-fry for 1 minute. Add the courgettes and spices, and cook for 2 minutes. Add the coconut cream and bring to the boil, then add the peas and spinach, and cook until the spinach has wilted. Fold in the cooked tofu and coriander and season to taste. Serve with naan bread or rice.

Antony's tip For a more substantial stew, you can add loads of other vegetables to this dish.

Serves 4

250g (9oz) firm tofu, well drained and cut into 2.5cm (1in) pieces

6 tbsp olive oil

1 onion, roughly chopped

2 cloves garlic, finely chopped

1 red medium-hot chilli, finely sliced

2.5cm (1in) ginger, peeled and grated

1 courgette, cut into 1cm (½in) dice

½ tsp ground turmeric

½ tsp ground cumin

6 tbsp thick coconut cream

115g (4oz) petits pois

2 handfuls of spinach, washed

2 tbsp chopped coriander

TO SERVE
Naan bread or boiled rice

Vegetarians are so easy to cook for – as long as they're not the nut-roast variety! I'm not a veggie, but I'll regularly have a bowl of this delicious curry. This recipe also lends itself to being served with grilled meat or fish. Oops. Sorry, vegetarians!

Vegetable Curry in a Flash

Timetable: from start to table in 25 minutes
Preparation 10 minutes | Cooking 15 minutes

In a saucepan, cook the onion and garlic in olive oil for 3 minutes. Meanwhile, use a food processor to mix the ground cumin, coriander and turmeric, chilli powder, coriander and mint leaves with a splash of water to make a smooth paste. Add this mixture to the onions and cook for 2 minutes.

Add the courgettes, mushrooms, peppers, tomatoes and sultanas, and cook for 8 minutes, adding a little tomato juice if required. Fold in the garam masala and lemon juice, cook for 1 minute and season to taste. Top with a dollop of yogurt and scatter with the flaked almonds. Serve with rice.

Antony's tip Add a drained can of chickpeas, some shredded cabbage, some butternut squash or an aubergine for a more substantial curry.

Serves 4

1 onion, finely chopped

2 cloves garlic, finely chopped

90ml (3fl oz) good olive oil

1 tsp ground cumin

1 tsp ground coriander

1 tsp ground turmeric

½ tsp ground chilli powder

Half a bunch of coriander

12 mint leaves

2 courgettes, cut into 1cm (½ in) dice

115g (4oz) button mushrooms, quartered

4 roasted red peppers, from a shop-bought jar, chopped

400g (14oz) can chopped tomatoes, drained

2 tbsp sultanas

1 tsp garam masala

Juice of 1 lemon

TO SERVE

175ml (6fl oz) Greek yogurt

2 tbsp toasted almond flakes

Boiled rice

Real Egg Curry

I used to have egg curry when I was at school, and if I remember correctly, it was pretty grim! However, Ed Baines made one on *Saturday Cooks* and it was delicious, so I decided to give it another go. This is a great recipe for vegetarians.

Timetable: from start to table in 40 minutes
Preparation 15 minutes | Cooking 25 minutes

Heat the butter or ghee in a large saucepan or frying pan, and cook the onions and garlic for 2 minutes.

In a food processor, blitz together the coriander and all the spices with a splash of water until you have a fine paste. Add this to the onions along with the sugar, and cook for a couple of minutes.

Add all the vegetables except the peas, then add the stock and cook over a medium heat for 20 minutes, adding extra stock if required. In the last 5 minutes of cooking, add the peas and eggs. Season to taste, and serve with a dollop of Greek yogurt on a bed of pilau rice.

Antony's tip Feel free to play with the vegetables in this recipe: cauliflower, pumpkin, courgettes and spinach all go down well. For good presentation, halve the eggs, placing them on top of the curry, cut side up.

Serves 4

85g (3oz) unsalted butter or ghee

1 onion, roughly chopped

2 cloves garlic, finely chopped

1 bunch of coriander

1 tsp cumin

1 tsp garam masala

1 tsp chat masala (optional)

1 tsp turmeric

1 tsp chilli powder

1 tsp caster sugar

6 tomatoes, roughly chopped

1 sweet potato, peeled and cut into 2cm (¾ in) cubes

1 aubergine, cut into 2cm (¾ in) cubes, or 325g (12oz) mini aubergines

1 large floury potato, cut into 2cm (¾ in) cubes

300ml (10fl oz) vegetable stock

225g (8oz) frozen petits pois

6 hard-boiled eggs, shelled

Salt and ground black pepper

TO SERVE

175ml (6fl oz) Greek yogurt

Pilau rice

This is my favourite chapter in the book, with loads of yummy dishes that should appeal to the entire family. There's a mixture of 'naughty-but-nice' and 'healthy-but-delicious' dishes, and all of them can be knocked up in a flash.

You can opt for a trendy dish such as the Caesar Salad Sandwich or the Spiced Seared Squid with a Light Crunchy Salad, but for the most part these are adaptations of dishes that I used to enjoy as a child. Of course, now we have a far greater choice of ingredients, and this, in turn, translates into a more exciting range of ideas.

In this chapter, I've used some canned products, which I think are often underrated. One of the oldest forms of preserving, canning is, in my opinion, also one of the purest, with most products being canned in oil or salted water and void of chemicals and additives.

soups, salads & snacks

Featuring lots of lovely, fresh, Oriental flavours, this recipe is another great way of using up your leftover Sunday roast. If you don't have any leftovers, you can buy cooked pork in the deli or supermarket.

Leftover Pork Noodle Soup

Timetable: from start to table in 20 minutes
Preparation 10 minutes | Cooking 10 minutes

Cook the noodles according to the manufacturer's directions, refresh them under cold water, then drain and set aside.

Heat the two oils in a large wok, add the garlic, ginger and chilli, and cook over a high heat for 1 minute. Add the chicken stock, soy sauce and honey, and bring to the boil.

Add the sugar snaps and broccoli, and return to the boil. Add the pork and spinach leaves, and cook for 2 minutes. Fold in the spring onions and coriander.

Divide the noodles between four large hot bowls and spoon over the soup. Serve with lime wedges.

Serves 4

175g (6oz) fine egg noodles

1 tbsp vegetable oil

1 tsp sesame oil

2 cloves garlic, chopped

2.5cm (1in) ginger, peeled and grated

½ tsp chilli flakes

1.8 litres (3 pints) chicken stock

3 tbsp light soy sauce

1 tsp clear honey

85g (3oz) sugar snaps

85g (3oz) tiny broccoli florets

175g (6oz) cooked pork, shredded

1 handful of baby spinach leaves

4 spring onions, thinly sliced

2 tbsp coriander leaves

TO SERVE
Lime wedges

Mussel, Bacon and Potato Chowder

One-pot lunches, such as good chunky soups, represent excellent value. In addition, they are filling and delicious, and they save on the washing-up! There's a naughty creaminess about this dish, but on the other hand, it's a great way of getting the children to eat fish.

Timetable: from start to table in 40 minutes
Preparation 15 minutes | Cooking 25 minutes

Cook the shallot, garlic and thyme in boiling cider in a large covered saucepan for about 5 minutes. Add the mussels (discard any open ones that don't close when you tap them on the side of the sink), cover and cook until they open – about 3–4 minutes. Throw away any that don't open. Drain in a colander reserving the cooking liquid separately from the mussels. When the mussels are cool enough to handle, remove their shells. (You can leave some in the shell for garnish if you want.)

Meanwhile, heat the butter in the empty mussel pan, add the bacon and onion, and cook for 5 minutes, until the bacon is crisping and the onion softening.

Mix the retained cooking liquid with the stock, then add the leeks, potatoes, carrots and celery. Simmer until the vegetables are tender; if you like your chowder a little thicker, mash some of the potatoes into the liquid.

Add the milk and cream, and bring to simmering point, then add the fish and cook for 3 minutes. Return the mussels to the chowder, along with the parsley, and season to taste.

Antony's tip Try a sliced bulb of fennel instead of celery and carrots, or replace the cider with dry white wine, adding a splash of Pernod towards the end of cooking.

Serves 4

1 shallot, finely chopped

1 clove garlic, finely chopped

1 tsp soft thyme leaves

300ml (10fl oz) dry cider

1kg (2¼lb) mussels, cleaned

25g (1oz) unsalted butter

200g (7oz) smoked bacon or pancetta lardons

1 onion, roughly chopped

300ml (10fl oz) vegetable or fish stock

2 leeks, washed and sliced into 2.5cm (1in) rings

225g (8oz) floury potatoes, peeled and cut into 2.5cm (1in) dice

2 carrots, peeled and sliced

2 sticks of celery, de-strung and sliced

300ml (10fl oz) full-fat milk

150ml (5fl oz) double cream

450g (1lb) white fish fillets, such as pollack or whiting, cut into 5cm (2in) pieces

2 tbsp chopped parsley

Salt and ground black pepper

Once upon a time a chilli pepper was just a chilli pepper. You never knew what strength to expect: it either blew your head off or made you wonder what all the fuss was about. It is quite the opposite in America, where you are offered more than 100 varieties of chilli, rated for spiciness from 1 to 10. Recently, enterprising suppliers have started a similar process over here in the United Kingdom, and different chilli varieties can now be found in our supermarkets, too.

Chicken, Chilli and Corn Soup

Timetable: from start to table in 35 minutes
Preparation 10 minutes | Cooking 25 minutes

Pan-fry the chillies, bacon, onion and garlic in the butter until the onion is soft – about 5 minutes.

Add the remaining ingredients except the double cream. Simmer, covered, for 20 minutes.

Season to taste and finish with the double cream.

Antony's tip If you have difficulty finding fresh jalapeño chillies, replace them with long red or green Dutch ones.

Serves 4

4 jalapeño (medium to hot strength) chillies, seeded and finely diced

4 rashers of smoked streaky bacon, diced

1 onion, finely diced

1 clove garlic, finely diced

55g (2oz) unsalted butter

1 tsp soft thyme leaves

1 medium-sized potato, peeled and finely diced

4 boneless chicken thighs, skinned and diced

225g (8oz) fresh, frozen or canned corn niblets

1.2 litres (2 pints) chicken stock

150ml (5fl oz) double cream

Salt and ground black pepper

Oriental Bean Salad
Whether or not you eat meat, we all need to take a break from heavy proteins from time to time. This recipe gives lunch in a flash, with under 200 calories per serving.

Timetable: from start to table in 15 minutes
Preparation 15 minutes

Combine the ingredients for the salad in a bowl.

To make the dressing, combine the ingredients in a clean jam jar, tighten the lid and shake well. If time permits, allow the flavours to develop for half an hour.

Dress the salad just before serving.

Antony's tip Any type of canned beans will work just as well as cannellini beans.

Serves 4

FOR THE SALAD

2 x 400g (14oz) cans cannellini beans, drained and rinsed

150g (5oz) salad greens of your choice

1 small bunch of spring onions, sliced

1 small bunch of coriander, roughly chopped

12 mint leaves, shredded

6 basil leaves, ripped

FOR THE DRESSING

1 tsp grated ginger

1 tbsp sesame oil

2 tbsp soy sauce or tamari

2 tbsp sweet chilli sauce

Juice and grated zest of 2 limes

This combination of great Mediterranean flavours is perfect for vegetarians or for anyone who wants to cut back on their protein intake. The salad is easy to put together, and the fried halloumi really adds another dimension.

Pan-Fried Halloumi with Fattoush Salad

Timetable: from start to table in 25 minutes
Preparation 15 minutes | Cooking 10 minutes

Preheat the oven to 170°C/340°F/Gas 3. Place the pitta wedges on a flat oven tray and cook until crisp – about 8 minutes. Drizzle with a little olive oil and rub gently with the garlic.

Meanwhile, toss together the cucumber, tomatoes, red onion, parsley and paprika. Combine two tablespoons of the oil with the lemon juice, salt and pepper, then crush the garlic and add it to the dressing.

Heat a frying pan with the remaining oil, then sprinkle the cheese with cumin and fry the slices until golden on both sides – about 6 minutes.

Toss the salad with the crisp pitta and the dressing. Place on four plates and top each with two slices of halloumi.

Antony's tip This salad is the perfect accompaniment to grilled lamb, too. All you need to do is replace the parsley with a few shredded mint leaves.

Serves 4

1 large pitta bread, halved horizontally, then cut into wedges

4 tbsp extra virgin olive oil

1 clove garlic

Half a cucumber, peeled, seeded and cut into 0.5cm (¼in) half moons

2 good tomatoes, seeded and roughly cut

1 red onion, halved then thinly sliced

Half a bunch of flat-leaf parsley, leaves only

½ tsp sweet paprika

60ml (2fl oz) lemon juice

Salt and ground black pepper

225g (8oz) halloumi cheese, cut into 8 slices

½ tsp ground cumin

Sardine and Potato Salad

I have to own up to a penchant for some canned goods. In fact, my life is sometimes dominated by Heinz, what with its tomato soup and baked beans, and that's without mentioning the love affair I have with its ketchup! One of the canned products in my larder is vintage sardines, stored at least ten years before eating, and lovingly turned every two months. Yeah, right…

Timetable: from start to table in under 25 minutes
Preparation 10 minutes | Cooking 12 minutes

Serves 4

450g (1lb) waxy new potatoes
2 x 120g (4oz) cans sardines in oil
3 tbsp extra virgin olive oil
2 tsp lemon juice
1 tsp Dijon mustard
Salt and ground black pepper
1 handful of crisp salad leaves
3 spring onions, sliced
1 tbsp mayonnaise

Boil the potatoes in salted water until tender. Drain and thinly slice while still warm.

While the potatoes are cooking, whisk together the oil from the sardines, the extra virgin olive oil, lemon juice and mustard. Season with salt and ground black pepper.

Mix the warm potatoes with the dressing, and arrange on the crisp salad leaves.

Meanwhile, mash the sardines and combine them with the spring onions, mayonnaise and plenty of black pepper.

Serve on top of the warm potato salad.

Antony's tip You can replace the sardines with any type of canned or smoked fish, such as mackerel or trout.

Something Bright for Summer
Ready to use and convenient, canned tuna is a must in any store cupboard, whether you use it for quick sandwiches, a pasta dish or a fishcake. Salads, while not always popular in our household, are a necessity from time to time, so this colourful number fits the bill.

Timetable: from start to table in under 15 minutes
Preparation 12 minutes

For the dressing, place all the ingredients in a clean jam jar and shake together vigorously.

Combine all the salad ingredients, add enough dressing to coat and gently toss together.

Antony's tip If you're into canned food, try replacing the tuna with salmon, sardines or Alaskan crab.

Serves 4

FOR THE SALAD

2 x 185g (6oz) cans tuna in oil, drained

400g (14oz) can white cannellini beans, drained and rinsed

1 small red onion, halved and thinly sliced

1 punnet yellow or red cherry tomatoes, each halved

10 basil leaves, ripped

1 Hass avocado, peeled, stoned and cut into wedges

1 handful of rocket leaves

FOR THE DRESSING

3 tbsp extra virgin olive oil

2 tsp good balsamic vinegar

Juice and grated zest of 1 lemon

1 tsp caster sugar

1 tsp Dijon mustard

1 tsp shop-bought pesto

Salt and ground black pepper

We all love deep-fried calamari (squid) rings. This seared-squid dish packs just as much flavour, while being far healthier.

Spiced Seared Squid with a Light Crunchy Salad

Timetable: from start to table in 20 minutes
Preparation 15 minutes | Cooking 5 minutes

Cut the squid tubes along their length on one side to open them up flat, then, using a sharp knife, score the inside of each tube in a tight diamond pattern without cutting all the way through. Cut each tube into pieces – four to six depending on its size.

Combine the squid pieces with the pepper, salt, lime juice and zest, and allow to marinate for 5 minutes.

Meanwhile, combine all the dry salad ingredients in one bowl. Mix the wet salad ingredients in another bowl to make the dressing. Just before serving, toss the salad with the dressing.

Heat the oil in a wok or large frying pan until almost smoking, then add the squid pieces, scored side down. Cook for 1 minute, then turn and cook for a further 45 seconds. They will curl once turned over. Remove and serve with the salad.

Antony's tip Try to buy medium-sized squid because baby squid shrinks to nothing. Large ones are best used for stewing. It's important to cook the squid for only a short period of time to prevent it from becoming tough.

Serves 4

FOR THE SQUID

450g (1lb) squid tubes, cleaned

½ tsp Sichuan peppercorns, crushed

1 tsp salt (Maldon)

Juice and zest of 1 lime

1 tbsp non-flavoured oil

FOR THE SALAD

Half a cucumber, peeled, seeded and diced

3 spring onions, sliced

1 avocado, peeled, stoned and diced

1 green pepper, seeded and cut into 1cm (½ in) dice

12 mint leaves, shredded

2 tbsp roughly chopped coriander leaves

Juice and grated zest of 1 lime

1 tsp fish sauce (nam pla)

2 tsp clear honey

It's a hot day, and you can't be bothered to spend an eternity at the stove. You fancy something quick and easy, so you turn to the larder and spot a can of salmon. Well, this is what you can do with it…

Cheat's Thai-Style Salmon Salad

Timetable: from start to table in 15 minutes
Preparation 15 minutes

Place all the ingredients for the dressing in a clean jam jar and shake to combine.

Mix the cucumber, shallots, cherry tomatoes, carrots and herbs, and toss with enough dressing to coat.

Arrange four pieces of gem lettuce at the bottom of each of four bowls and top with the dressed salad. Then break up the salmon and scatter over the top. Drizzle over any remaining dressing.

Antony's tip This excellent salad also works with leftover roast beef or chicken.

Serves 4

FOR THE SALAD

Half a cucumber, peeled, seeded and cut into 1cm (½ in) chunks

3 shallots, thinly sliced

200g (7oz) cherry tomatoes, halved

1 carrot, peeled and very finely sliced

12 mint leaves, shredded

1 small bunch of coriander, roughly chopped

2 baby gem lettuces, each cut into 8 wedges

1 large can (418g/14oz) Alaska wild salmon, drained

FOR THE DRESSING

Juice of 3 limes

1 tbsp soy sauce or tamari

1 tsp ketcap manis

1 tsp soft dark brown sugar

1 tbsp sweet chilli sauce

Autumn Bliss With our messed-up weather system, we often get warm days in autumn. When that happens, a salad made with delicious seasonal ingredients such as pears and walnuts is just the thing to serve. This is lovely, light and simple.

Timetable: from start to table in 15 minutes
Preparation 15 minutes

Place all the ingredients for the dressing in a clean jam jar and shake vigorously. Season to taste.

Combine all the salad ingredients except the cheese. Add enough dressing to cover and toss to combine. Divide between four plates, then scatter with the blue cheese.

Antony's tip If you like smoked mackerel or trout, feel free to use either instead of smoked chicken. If you can't find smoked chicken breasts, try smoked turkey slices instead.

Serves 2

FOR THE SALAD

1 bag of watercress, large stalks removed

1 head of baby gem lettuce, leaves separated and ripped if large

2 smoked chicken breasts, skinless and thinly sliced

2 Conference pears, peeled, cored and cut into wedges

25g (1oz) walnut pieces

55g (2oz) crumbled blue cheese (Roquefort, Stilton or Beenleigh Blue)

FOR THE DRESSING

3 tsp aged red wine vinegar

2 tbsp extra virgin olive oil

1 tbsp walnut oil (optional)

¼ tsp caster sugar

1 tsp Dijon mustard

Salt and ground black pepper

This lovely light salad should please the entire family – so long as they like coconut, that is! I tend to serve it at room temperature, but you may prefer it more chilled.

Cool Coconut Chicken

Timetable: from start to table in 20 minutes
Preparation 10 minutes | Cooking 10 minutes, plus cooling time

Place the lemongrass, juice of two limes, all the zest, sugar and coconut milk in a saucepan. Bring to the boil, then reduce the heat and simmer for 10 minutes. Remove from the heat and cool as quickly as possible.

Cut the chicken into shreds and toss with the sesame oil and remaining lime juice. Season.

Combine all the salad ingredients, add the chicken and enough dressing to coat generously. Serve immediately.

Antony's tip Don't chop the herbs until you are about to put the salad together (Step 3), since they tend to go black if chopped too early.

Serves 4

2 tbsp finely chopped lemongrass, tough outer stem removed

Juice and grated zest of 3 limes

2 tsp soft light brown sugar

240ml (8fl oz) thick coconut milk

2 cooked chicken breasts or 450g (1lb) leftover roast chicken

2 tsp sesame oil

Salt and ground black pepper

FOR THE SALAD

24 mint leaves, roughly chopped

Half a bunch of coriander, roughly chopped

A bunch of watercress, tough stems discarded

Half a cucumber, peeled and thinly sliced

2 tsp sesame seeds

4 spring onions, sliced

Broad Bean and Courgette Drop Scones with Hot Smoked Salmon

My children love pancakes of any description, and these little bites work a treat. The scones are also a great way to get them to eat their vegetables.

Timetable: from start to table in 25 minutes
Preparation 15 minutes | Cooking 10 minutes

Slice the courgette lengthways with a vegetable peeler to produce courgette ribbons.

Combine the chilli flakes, water and caster sugar and cook over a medium heat until the sugar dissolves, then reduce the mixture by one-third, until syrupy. Add the vinegar and bring to the boil. Add the courgette ribbons and cook for 30 seconds. Drain and set aside.

To make the scones, sieve the flour and bicarbonate of soda into a bowl with a pinch of salt and pepper, then whisk in the buttermilk and egg yolk. Fold in the broad beans, grated courgette and chives.

Beat the two egg whites until soft peaks form, then fold them into the batter. Divide the mixture into four. Oil a large non-stick frying pan (or two smaller ones) and place on a medium heat, then spoon the mixture into the pan to make four circular drop scones. When small bubbles start appearing on the surface of the scone, after about 2 minutes, flip over and cook for a further 2 minutes. Keep warm.

Meanwhile, cook the smoked salmon at full power in the microwave for 45 seconds.

Place a scone on each of four warmed plates, flake the salmon on top, and finish with pickled courgettes and a little soured cream or crème fraîche.

Antony's tip 'Hot' smoked salmon is available in supermarkets and looks like cooked salmon. It comes in fillets, as opposed to 'cold' smoked salmon, which tends to be thinly sliced.

Serves 4

450g (1lb) 'hot' smoked salmon

FOR THE PICKLED COURGETTES

1 large courgette, topped and tailed

1 pinch dried chilli flakes

60ml (2fl oz) water

55g (2oz) caster sugar

60ml (2fl oz) cider vinegar

FOR THE SCONES

175g (6oz) self-raising flour

½ tsp bicarbonate of soda

Salt and ground white pepper

A carton (284ml/10fl oz) of buttermilk

1 free-range egg, separated, plus 1 egg white

115g (4oz) baby broad beans, defrosted

1 medium-sized courgette, grated

2 tbsp snipped chives

Oil for greasing

TO SERVE

Soured cream or crème fraîche

This salad is reminiscent of coronation chicken, but with a couple of add-ons. It is a great way of using up the Sunday roast leftovers, or it can be prepared with a ready-cooked chicken. This classic recipe deserves to be maintained and it is also great for introducing children to new flavours.

Curried Chicken Salad

Timetable: from start to table in 15 minutes
Preparation 10 minutes | Cooking 5 minutes

Cook the onions over a medium heat in the oil for 5 minutes; add the curry paste, tomato purée and apricot jam, and stir to combine. Allow to cool.

Combine the onion mixture with the mayonnaise and soured cream. In a separate bowl, combine the remaining ingredients, then add enough of the dressing to coat liberally. Serve on watercress or baby gem lettuce leaves.

Antony's tip This recipe also works well substituting prawns for chicken. Alternatively, try it with smoked chicken and some diced celery.

Serves 4

1 onion, finely chopped

1 tbsp olive oil

1 tbsp madras curry paste

½ tbsp tomato purée

1 tbsp apricot jam

150ml (5fl oz) good mayonnaise

4 tbsp soured cream

55g (2oz) broken walnut pieces

1 Cox or Granny Smith apple, cored and cut into wedges

1 carrot, peeled and grated

325g (12oz) cooked chicken, ripped or cut into chunks

TO SERVE

Watercress or baby gem lettuce leaves

Caesar Salad Sandwich
Every year I used to look forward to our meagre ration of British sun, but in recent times, rationing has gone by the board and we've been given a full diet of sun, sun, sun. Hot weather is not conducive to pigging out, so I should be as thin as a rake. I'm not, and that may be due to the fact that I eat too many Caesar salad sandwiches!

Timetable: from start to table in 20 minutes | Preparation 5 minutes | Cooking and construction 15 minutes

Fold the garlic, anchovies, lemon zest and grated Parmesan into the mayonnaise. Spread most of this mayonnaise on each side of the rolls or on each slice of bread and toss the cos lettuce with the rest.

Top half of each roll with the lettuce, then with the Parmesan shavings, which are created by drawing a potato peeler over a chunk of fresh Parmesan, then finally the egg slices.

Season with plenty of black pepper, and assemble the sandwich by topping with the remaining bread. Cut each sandwich in half and enjoy!

Antony's tip Here's a tip for the perfect boiled eggs. Immediately after draining the boiling water, cover the eggs with cold water and a few ice cubes, and leave them until completely cool. This speeds up the process and stops a dark grey-green ring forming around the yolks.

Serves 4

2 cloves garlic, crushed with a little salt

4 canned anchovies, finely chopped

1 tbsp grated lemon zest

25g (1oz) grated Parmesan cheese

300ml (10fl oz) mayonnaise

4 large wholegrain brown rolls, halved, or 8 slices wholegrain brown bread

Half a cos lettuce, ripped into bite-sized pieces

Fresh Parmesan cheese shavings

4 hard-boiled eggs, peeled and sliced

Freshly ground black pepper

I was given a similar sandwich by Robyn Roux, the wife of Michel Roux Sr, who has held three Michelin stars for longer than any other chef in the UK. Chefs love this sort of food. It takes a bit of doing but it's worth the effort.

The Kitchen-Sink Club Sandwich

Timetable: from start to table in 35 minutes
Preparation 15 minutes | Cooking 18–20 minutes

Preheat the oven to 200°C/390°F/Gas 6, and place a large flat baking tray inside to heat up.

Heat the oil in an ovenproof frying pan. Add the tomatoes, season with salt and pepper, and cook for 5 minutes over a medium heat. Put the bacon rashers on top of the tomatoes and place in the oven for 6 minutes.

Meanwhile, in a bowl, mash the avocados, retaining some texture, then add the onion, chilli, spices, lime juice and coriander. Season.

Lay the bread slices on your work surface. On four slices, spread the avocado mixture; on the other four slices, spread the mayonnaise. Place two rashers of bacon on each avocado slice, followed by two slices of tomato, the mozzarella slices and the chicken. Place the mayonnaise bread slices, mayo side down, on top of the chicken. You now have four sandwiches. Butter the top slices of bread on the outside, then grind over a little pepper.

Place the sandwiches butter side down onto your hot baking tray, and butter and pepper what is now the top of the sandwich. Put the sandwiches in the oven and cook until the mozzarella is melting and the outside of the sandwich is golden – about 7 minutes. Slice each sandwich into four triangles and serve.

Serves 4

1 tbsp olive oil

2 beefsteak tomatoes, each cut into 4 slices

Salt and ground black pepper

8 rashers of back bacon, rinds removed

2 ripe avocados, peeled and stoned

Half a red onion, finely diced

1 red chilli, finely diced

½ tsp ground cumin

½ tsp ground coriander

Juice of 1 lime

2 tbsp chopped coriander

Salt and ground black pepper

8 slices white bread, thickly sliced

2 tbsp mayonnaise

2 balls of cows' mozzarella, each cut into 8 slices and seasoned with salt and pepper

2 cooked chicken breasts, thinly sliced

55g (2oz) unsalted butter, softened

Antony's tip If you're making just one or two sandwiches, you can fry the outside slices before construction begins.

Gruyère Beignets with Crisp Apples

I think we tread a dangerous path when we try to reduce saturated fat for everyone – it's never a good idea to generalize across the board. Children need their cheese, because they need calcium to develop strong bones. You shouldn't make this dish every day, but it's fine to serve it once in a while, as part of a balanced diet. Most importantly, these beignets go down a treat. Get the children to take a bite of apple, immediately followed by a bite of cheese. Magic!

Timetable: from start to table in 15 minutes
Preparation 10 minutes | Cooking 5 minutes

Preheat 5cm (2in) of vegetable oil in a wok or large saucepan. If you have a cooking thermometer, the temperature should reach 180°C (360°F). Better still, buy yourself an electric deep-fat fryer, which is thermostatically controlled.

Cut the cheese into rectangles that are roughly the dimensions of two fingers. Dip these shapes into the dusting flour.

Tip the flour into a bowl and beat the egg into it, then add the baking powder and beat in the wine until the mixture achieves the thickness of single cream. (If you're worried about using alcohol, replace the wine with apple juice or half milk and half water.)

One by one, dip the Gruyère rectangles into the batter, then into the hot oil. Cook them until they have swollen and become golden – about 5 minutes. You may need to fry them in batches, in which case keep the cooked ones warm in a low oven. Drain on kitchen paper, then sprinkle with salt and pepper.

Serve the beignets with cored wedges of crisp apple.

Antony's tip Experiment with different cheeses, such as Cheddar or mozzarella.

Serves 4

Vegetable oil for frying

325g (12oz) Gruyère cheese

175g (6oz) plain flour, plus a little extra for dusting

1 free-range egg

½ tsp baking powder

150ml (5fl oz) dry white wine

Salt and ground black pepper

TO SERVE

4 Cox apples, cored and cut into wedges

We like cauliflower cheese and we like cheese on toast, so why not combine the two? My friend Merrilees Parker reckons this is her recipe, while I maintain it's mine. I guess we'll have to fight it out one day! It doesn't really matter, though, for this is very pleasant – and so is Merrilees.

Cauliflower Cheese on Toast

Timetable: from start to table in 20 minutes
Preparation 5 minutes | Cooking 15 minutes

Preheat the grill to hot.

Place the cauliflower in a glass bowl, add one tablespoon of water, cover with clingfilm and blast in the microwave on full power for 4 minutes. Keep warm.

Meanwhile, place the Cheddar cheese, beer (if using), Worcestershire sauce, mustard and crème fraîche in a non-stick saucepan over a low heat, and stir until you have a smooth sauce. Remove from the heat and add the egg yolks. Stir to combine and season to taste.

Drain the cauliflower of any moisture, then mash it to form a very rough purée. Season, then fold in enough of the cheese sauce to bind the cauliflower. Spoon onto the untoasted side of the bread and place under the grill until golden brown – about 2 minutes.

Antony's tip The cheese mixture can be made in advance. If you take this route, then I suggest you preheat the oven to 200°C/390°F/Gas 6 and cook the bread and topping for 10 minutes. If you are a very strict vegetarian, you might want to leave out the Worcestershire sauce.

Serves 4

1 small cauliflower, broken into small florets

175g (6oz) mature Cheddar cheese, grated

1 splash of beer (optional)

1 tsp Worcestershire sauce

2 tsp English mustard

4 tbsp crème fraîche

2 free-range egg yolks

Salt and ground black pepper

4 slices of crusty wholemeal bread, toasted on one side only

Interesting Sardines on Toast Canned sardines
are a great way of eating one portion of oily fish. And they're delicious.

Timetable: from start to table in 15 minutes
Preparation 10 minutes | Cooking 5 minutes

Brush the bread slices with the olive oil, then cook them on a griddle
pan on one side only. Place each slice, toasted side down, on a plate.

Combine the remaining ingredients, except the rocket leaves,
breaking up the sardines. Season to taste.

Place the rocket leaves on the grilled bread, then top with the sardines.

Antony's tip Serve your sardines whole on top of
the egg mix for a more classic presentation.

Serves 4

4 slices of country bread
1 tbsp extra virgin olive oil
8 canned sardines
2 hard-boiled eggs, chopped
(see tip on page 151)
2 roasted red peppers, from
a shop-bought jar, chopped
1 tbsp capers, chopped
4 canned anchovies, chopped
Leaves from half a bunch of
parsley, roughly chopped
6 basil leaves, shredded
1 tbsp white wine vinegar
A handful of rocket leaves
Salt and ground black pepper

Pitta Pride If you go to Greece, be sure to buy a souvlaki from a
street vendor. I've come up with a delicious alternative. Prepare to get messy!

Timetable: from start to table in 25 minutes
Preparation 10 minutes | Cooking 15 minutes

Preheat the oven to 160°C/320°F/Gas 2.

In a frying pan over a medium heat, fry the onion and garlic in the oil
until softening – about 5 minutes. Add the mince and break it up with
a wooden spoon. Fold in the chilli powder, tomato paste, paprika,
coriander, cinnamon and cumin. Cook for 10 minutes, stirring regularly.

Meanwhile, cut a pocket in each of the pitta breads and place in the
oven for 5 minutes. When warm, open up the pocket and stuff it with
the lettuce and red onion, followed by the mince, then drizzle with
the yogurt and sprinkle with the mint. Serve immediately.

Serves 4

1 Spanish onion, chopped
2 cloves garlic, finely chopped
1 tbsp good olive oil
225g (8oz) lamb mince
¼ tsp chilli powder
2 tsp sun-dried tomato paste
½ tsp each smoked paprika,
ground coriander and ground
cinnamon
1 tsp ground cumin
4 large pitta breads
4 tbsp shredded
iceberg-lettuce leaves
Half a red onion, finely sliced
2 tbsp Greek yogurt
1 tbsp shredded mint

Potato Pizza with Onion, Bacon and Melting Cheese

This recipe revolves around a really simple idea, but it manages to wow the entire family. Once you've made the potato bases, the choice of topping is entirely yours.

Timetable: from start to table in 45 minutes
Preparation 15 minutes | Cooking 30 minutes

Preheat the oven to 180°C/360°F/Gas 4.

Coarsely grate the potatoes, rinse in salted water, then drain and squeeze them dry. Mix the potatoes with the melted butter, salt and pepper. Arrange four circles of potato in one large frying pan (or two smaller ones). Fry over a medium heat for 5 minutes, then pop into the oven for 15 minutes.

Meanwhile, in another frying pan, cook the onions in hot oil for 5 minutes until they start to change colour. Add the bacon, mushrooms and thyme, and cook for a further 5 minutes, until the bacon starts to crisp.

Spoon the bacon mix on top of the potato bases, then top each with two slices of mozzarella and a couple of grinds of black pepper. Sprinkle with Parmesan and return to the oven for 8–10 minutes, until the cheese is bubbling and golden. Serve immediately with salad.

Antony's tip In this instance I use bacon, but it could easily be chicken or leftover roast, or how about a dollop of your favourite tomato sauce before you top the potato bases with cheese? Go wild with your own recipe imagination!

Serves 4

675g (1½ lb) floury potatoes, peeled

85g (3oz) melted butter

Salt and ground black pepper

1 onion, finely diced

1 tbsp olive oil

175g (6oz) smoked bacon or pancetta lardons

115g (4oz) button mushrooms, sliced

1 tsp soft thyme leaves

1 ball of cows' mozzarella, cut into 8 slices

40g (1½ oz) grated Parmesan cheese

I like the idea of a quesadilla, or tortilla sandwich, but the fillings can often be a bit dull. I hope you'll find my suggestions a little more satisfying.

Oozing Vegetable Quesadillas

Timetable: from start to table in under 25 minutes
Preparation 12 minutes | Cooking 12 minutes

Preheat the oven to 180°C/360°F/Gas 4.

In a food processor, blend together the ricotta, spinach, garlic and a few grindings of salt and pepper. Scrape the mixture out into a bowl and fold in the sweetcorn.

In another bowl, roughly mash the avocado, leaving some texture, then fold in the spices, spring onions, tomatoes, coriander and lime juice. Season to taste.

Lay four tortillas on a work surface, spread them with the spinach-and-cheese mix, then top with the avocado. Finally, sprinkle on the Cheddar cheese and drizzle with the sweet chilli sauce. Top the filling with another tortilla.

Place the tortilla sandwiches on two flat baking trays, then place four slices of mozzarella on top of each. Sprinkle with salt and pepper and put into the oven for 8–10 minutes. You can also brown under the grill for a minute or two if you like. Cut each into four wedges and serve immediately.

Antony's tip Non-vegetarians may want to put some crispy bacon in the tortillas as well, or perhaps some cooked chicken shreds.

Serves 4

150g (5oz) ricotta cheese

55g (2oz) cooked or frozen spinach, squeezed dry and chopped

1 clove garlic, sliced

Salt and ground black pepper

200g (7oz) can sweetcorn, drained

2 ripe avocados, peeled and stoned

½ tsp ground cumin

½ tsp ground coriander

1 medium-hot red chilli, finely chopped

3 spring onions, finely sliced

2 tomatoes, seeded and diced

2 tbsp chopped coriander

Juice of 1 lime

8 small soft-flour tortillas

115g (4oz) grated Cheddar cheese

3 tbsp sweet chilli sauce

2 balls of cows' mozzarella, each cut into 8 slices

'Leftovers' Crispy Pancakes When I was a child, the Sunday roast was always larger than it is today and, once cold, provided offerings for the rest of the week, in the form of cottage pie, curry and these cromeskis – crispy pancake rolls usually served with salad.

Timetable: from start to table in under 40 minutes
Preparation 15 minutes | Cooking 22–25 minutes

Place the onions in a saucepan with four tablespoons of water and the thyme leaves, and simmer gently for 12–15 minutes.

Heat half the butter in a frying pan, add the meat and the boiled onions with their juices, and cook for 3 minutes, stirring regularly. Fold in the herbs and season. Allow to cool, then fold in the egg yolk.

Meanwhile, in a bowl mix the ricotta, sultanas, honey and cinnamon.

Lay the pancakes on a work surface and spread a line of cream-cheese mixture on each one, leaving 2.5cm (1in) each side and 2.5cm (1in) in from the top of the pancake. Top the cream cheese with the meat mixture, then lightly roll up the pancakes, tucking them in at the sides.

Arrange three plates or shallow bowls: one with the flour, one with the beaten eggs and the last with the breadcrumbs. Dip each pancake roll in the flour, then the egg, then the breadcrumbs. Place them seam side down on a plate until ready to cook.

Preheat the oven to 180°C/360°F/Gas 4.

Heat the remaining butter in a large frying pan and fry the pancakes seam side down for 3 minutes, then turn them over and cook until golden. Put them in the oven until ready to serve – they should be very hot. Serve with salad or green vegetables.

Antony's tip You could also add any leftover cooked vegetables for a bubble-and-squeak-type parcel.

Serves 4

1 onion, finely chopped
1 tsp soft thyme leaves
55g (2oz) unsalted butter
300g (11oz) leftover roast beef, lamb or chicken, finely chopped
2 tbsp chopped parsley
1 tbsp snipped chives
Salt and ground black pepper
1 egg yolk and 2 free-range eggs, beaten
225g (8oz) ricotta or cream cheese
55g (2oz) sultanas
1 tbsp clear honey
A pinch of cinnamon
8 shop-bought pancakes
85g (3oz) plain seasoned flour
150g (5oz) white breadcrumbs

TO SERVE
Salad or green vegetables

puddings

Who can resist a pudding? The problem is that, in many cases, we have to resist ever-expanding waistlines. However, puddings also have a wonderfully comforting, curative effect; so there is definitely a need for them, albeit not too often. Children need puddings, they are an integral part of growing up.

The decision parents have to make is how often puddings should appear on the menu. It's all down to how active you are as a family. If you participate in regular sports, then the world is your pudding. If, on the other hand, you are glued to the TV, computer or games console, you might be a bit stuffed when it comes to enjoying a pud.

I've been criticized for creating the Snickers Pie, with its 1,200 calories per portion (but then it was invented for a children's party). It's actually no more calories than your kids might get from a meal of burger, fries and milkshake – a regular supper for many families. Once again, moderation is the key word: keep an eye on their waistlines and come to a decision.

Many of the puddings in this section aren't particularly healthy, but to any critics, I say, 'Chill'. I don't intend for them to be eaten on a daily basis. Puddings are fun and delicious, and there is a place for them, so enjoy my speedy selection occasionally, and when making them and eating them, please don't count the calories!

I know our waistlines don't allow us to eat pudding every day, so when you do treat yourself, keep it simple and make it delicious. This pudding is inspired by one cooked by Mary Berry on Daily Cooks.

Almondy Apple Pancakes with Almond Custard

Timetable: from start to table in 25 minutes
Preparation 10 minutes | Cooking 15 minutes

In a large frying pan, heat half the butter until foaming, then add the apple wedges and fry over a moderate heat until the apples are golden all over but still retain their shape. (Be careful, because Bramley apples collapse very quickly.) Fold in the brown sugar and toss to combine.

Lay the pancakes out on your work surface, then place the apples down each pancake, about one-third in. Sprinkle with almonds, grate over the marzipan and squeeze with a little lemon juice. Start to roll the pancakes, tucking in the sides, and make each one into a neat parcel. (Up to this point, the pancakes can be made ahead of time.)

Heat the remaining butter in a large frying pan and fry the pancake parcels over a medium heat until brown. Serve on warm plates.

Heat the custard in a saucepan or microwave, and fold in the almond essence or liqueur. Serve with the pancakes.

Antony's tip If you want a little more crunch to your apples, replace the Bramleys with Cox or Granny Smith varieties.

Serves 4

FOR THE PANCAKES

55g (2oz) unsalted butter

3 Bramley apples, each peeled, cored and cut into 12 wedges

115g (4oz) soft dark brown muscovado sugar

8 shop-bought crêpes or sweet pancakes

55g (2oz) toasted flaked almonds

115g (4oz) shop-bought marzipan

Juice of half a lemon

FOR THE CUSTARD

600ml (1 pint) best shop-bought fresh custard

1 tsp almond essence or extract or, for adults only, 2 tbsp amaretto almond liqueur

Autumn Fruit Amaretti Crumble Crumbles often
take the best part of an hour to produce, but not this one! It's all down to a
well-stocked store cupboard, so you can continue the age-old tradition of
cooking a lovely crumble for your children.

Timetable: from start to table in 30 minutes
Preparation 10 minutes | Cooking 20 minutes

Preheat the oven to 190°C/375°F/Gas 5.

Combine the fruit, apple sauce and cinnamon, and place the mixture
in a baking dish.

Combine the Amaretti biscuits, sugar, flour and ground almonds in
a bowl. Then, using your fingers or two knives, cut the butter into
the dry mixture until it creates crumbs. Sprinkle this mix over the
fruit together with the slivered almonds and bake uncovered until
bubbling and golden brown, about 15–20 minutes. Serve with
custard or ice cream.

Antony's tip Canning is a safe way of preserving foodstuffs
since it doesn't require loads of chemicals. I have a soft spot for many
canned products. Canned fruits are often particularly good, so try
a few different ones – gooseberries, apples, peaches, pineapple
and blackberries.

Serves 4

400g (14oz) can plums
in syrup, drained, halved
and stoned

400g (14oz) can pear halves,
drained and halved

250g (9oz) apple sauce

1 tsp ground cinnamon

85g (3oz) Amaretti biscuits,
crushed

55g (2oz) soft dark brown
sugar

40g (1½ oz) plain flour

25g (1oz) ground almonds

85g (3oz) unsalted butter

25g (1oz) blanched almonds,
sliced

TO SERVE

Custard or ice cream

I haven't had these fritters since I was a child, but I loved them then as much as my children love them now. This is an old-fashioned pud that has survived the test of time. Rings or wedges – the choice is yours.

Apple Fritters

Timetable: from start to table in under 15 minutes |Preparation 6 minutes |Cooking 6 minutes

Heat at least 5cm (2in) of oil in a wok until a cube of bread browns in 1 minute. If you have it, use an electric fryer set at 170°C (340°F).

Cut each apple into four rings or eight wedges. Beat the eggs in a bowl, beat in the flour, then dilute the mixture with milk and Kirsch (if using) – it should be the consistency of single cream. Add a pinch of salt.

Dip the apple rings, or wedges, in the batter, then carefully drop them in the hot oil. Cook them for approximately 3 minutes until golden, turning them over once. You may have to cook them in two batches.

Meanwhile, combine the sugar and cinnamon, and spoon the mixture onto a flat plate. As soon as you've lifted the fritters out of the oil, dip them into the spiced sugar. Serve immediately with custard, cream or ice cream.

Antony's tip Try the same recipe with acacia flowers, strawberries or banana slices instead of the apples.

Serves 4

Vegetable oil for frying

3 Granny Smith apples, peeled and cored

2 free-range eggs

3 tbsp plain flour

Up to 150ml (5fl oz) milk

60ml (2fl oz) Kirsch (optional)

Salt

3 tbsp caster sugar

1 tsp cinnamon

TO SERVE

Custard, cream or ice cream

Lemon Meringue Mess
Some of the loveliest food in the world looks a right mess, but in my opinion it doesn't really matter as long as the flavour is there. With this recipe, I just grab what I can from the store cupboard and fridge to make a delightful concoction.

Timetable: from start to table in under 15 minutes
Preparation 8 minutes | Cooking 5 minutes

Beat together the lemon curd and cream until you have soft peaks – be careful because cream mixed with anything acidic thickens quickly. Crumble half the meringues into the lemon cream. Cut the oranges between the membranes to create neat segments.

Place a scoop of ice cream in the base of each of four chilled tumblers, scatter with the orange segments and top with the lemon meringue mixture. Sprinkle the remaining broken meringue on top, followed by the lemon zest, and serve immediately.

Antony's tip Use this idea as a base for other flavours, such as chocolate and bananas, red fruits and orange liqueur, and toffee apple.

Serves 4

3 tbsp lemon curd

150ml (5fl oz) double cream

4 shop-bought meringue nests

2 oranges, peeled, pith removed

4 scoops vanilla ice cream

Grated zest of 1 unwaxed lemon

Hot Meringues with Orange Cream I was

inspired to create this easy, light pudding by a French dish called oeufs à la neige, or floating islands.

Timetable: from start to table in under 25 minutes
Preparation 10 minutes | Cooking 12 minutes

Preheat the oven to 160°C/320°F/Gas 2. Lightly butter four dariole moulds or ramekins, then sprinkle each with a little caster sugar. Shake out any sugar that does not stick to the butter.

To make the meringue, beat the egg whites with an electric whisk in a very clean bowl until soft peaks form. Then, continuing to beat, gradually add the sugar until the egg whites are stiff and glossy.

Divide the meringue between the four moulds and smooth the tops with the back of a wet teaspoon. Place the moulds in a deep-sided roasting tray and pour boiling water around them; the water should come halfway up the moulds. Place the tray in the heated oven and cook for 12 minutes, or until the meringue has risen by one-third and the top is light golden.

Meanwhile, combine the custard, double cream, orange zest and juice in a saucepan, then add the bay leaf and heat gently.

Arrange the orange slices in the bottom of four flat soup plates. When the meringues have cooked, allow them to rest in the water bath for 2 minutes before turning them out onto the centre of the orange slices. Spoon over the orange cream, discarding the bay leaf, and scatter with the chopped pistachios.

Antony's tip If you are preparing this pudding for adults only, you might want to add a little orange liqueur to the custard. Always beat egg whites at room temperature.

Serves 6

Butter for greasing
100g (3 ½ oz) caster sugar
3 egg whites
600ml (1 pint) finest shop-bought fresh custard
150ml (5fl oz) double cream
Grated zest of 1 organic orange
Juice of 2 organic oranges
1 bay leaf
2 organic oranges, peeled and thinly sliced
25g (1oz) chopped pistachios

Layered Banana Sundae
This is gobsmackingly good. Unfortunately, it is also gobsmackingly fattening, so approach with caution. It's kids' stuff that adults also enjoy. Just be sure you don't make it a habit!

Timetable: from start to table in 15 minutes
Preparation 10 minutes | Cooking 5 minutes

Serves 4

2 tbsp soft dark brown sugar

2 tbsp golden syrup

55g (2oz) unsalted butter

4 scoops caramel or vanilla ice cream

4 bananas

6 tbsp shop-bought fresh custard

150ml (5fl oz) whipping or double cream, beaten to semi-stiff peaks

25g (1oz) toasted flaked almonds

Heat together the sugar, syrup and butter until boiling and emulsified. Divide between four sundae glasses or tumblers, leaving some for a second layer and a final drizzle. Allow to cool slightly.

Place a scoop of ice cream onto the caramel. Add another layer of caramel and another scoop of ice cream, then top with the sliced bananas. Spoon over the custard, then the remaining banana slices.

Top with the whipped cream, then scatter over the almonds. Finally, drizzle over the remaining caramel sauce. Serve immediately.

Antony's tip You can go wild with this one! Try replacing the caramel sauce with chocolate sauce, or the bananas with raspberries. You can also fold broken meringue into the whipped cream.

Cheese and Pineapple ... And why not? Edouard de Pomaine suggests this classic combo in his brilliant book *Cooking in Ten Minutes*, and it really works well. Indeed, it is so simple that it should be made on a regular basis.

Timetable: from start to table in 5 minutes
Preparation 5 minutes (15 if using fresh pineapple)

Beat together the cream cheese, double cream, rum (if using) and icing sugar. Using an ice-cream scoop, place a cream-cheese ball in the centre of each of four plates and top with a slice of pineapple. Repeat and finish with a strawberry on the top.

Antony's tip You can also try this recipe with banana, mango or red fruits instead of pineapple.

Serves 4

225g (8oz) mild cream cheese or Philadelphia

90ml (3fl oz) double cream

1 tbsp dark rum (optional)

1 tbsp icing sugar

1 small pineapple, prepared and cut into 8 slices, or 8 rings of canned pineapple

4 strawberries, hulled

Banana and Pecan Drop Scones with Orange Syrup
When in Scotland, be sure to try the local drop scones, which are similar to American pancakes. With this recipe, I've had a little play and come up with a pudding that pleases the entire family.

Timetable: from start to table in 25 minutes
Preparation 5 minutes | Cooking 20 minutes

For the syrup, boil together the orange juice and sugar for 10–12 minutes, or until very syrupy. Allow to cool slightly, then fold in the orange liqueur (if using).

Mix together the plain flour, baking powder, mixed spice and icing sugar, then beat in the banana purée. Whisk the egg yolk and buttermilk together, then beat this mixture into the banana mix. Fold in the nuts and sultanas. Whisk the egg white to soft peaks and fold it in gently.

Heat a large non-stick frying pan, lightly browned with oil, and spoon tablespoons of the mixture into it, four at a time. Allow to cook for 1 minute, then top with two slices of banana and cook for another minute or so, until bubbles start appearing in the surface. Flip over and cook for a further 2 minutes until golden. Remove, keep warm and repeat with the rest. Serve on warm plates, topped with a little syrup and cream, or ice cream.

Antony's tip These drop scones taste great served American-style, with crispy bacon and maple syrup. For a more grown-up taste, try soaking the sultanas in rum. You can replace the bananas with apple purée and caramelized apple wedges.

Serves 4

FOR THE DROP SCONES

100g (3½oz) plain flour

1 tsp baking powder

½ tsp mixed spice

1 tbsp icing sugar

2 bananas, 1 sliced and 1 mashed until smooth

1 free-range egg, separated

120ml (4fl oz) buttermilk or Greek yogurt

55g (2oz) broken pecan nuts

40g (1½oz) sultanas

Vegetable oil for frying

FOR THE SYRUP

300ml (10fl oz) pulp-free fresh orange juice

150g (5oz) soft light brown sugar

2 tbsp orange liqueur (optional)

TO SERVE

Cream or ice cream

Cranachan
This very moreish Scottish pudding is made in a flash and appeals to the whole family – especially the adults, if you add a little malt whisky!

Timetable: from start to table in under 15 minutes
Preparation 10 minutes | Cooking 3–4 minutes

Preheat the oven to 200°C/390°F/Gas 6.

Lay the oats on a flat tray and place in the oven for 3–4 minutes, or until golden, tossing from time to time. Allow to cool.

Crush 115g (4oz) of raspberries with a potato masher, then push them through a fine sieve, discarding the seeds.

Beat the double cream to soft peaks, then fold in the honey, orange juice or whisky (if using) and all but 1 tablespoon of the toasted oats. Finally, swirl in the raspberry purée to create a ripple effect.

Divide half the raspberries between the bottom of each of the glasses, then put a layer of the oatmeal cream. Repeat, then place a few raspberries on the top and decorate with a mint leaf and the remaining oats.

Antony's tip Feel free to change the fruit according to what's in season. You can also try different honeys for a subtle taste change.

Serves 4

25g (1oz) medium oatmeal
325g (12oz) raspberries
300ml (10fl oz) double cream
3 tbsp clear heather honey
3 tbsp orange juice or malt whisky (optional)
mint leaves, to decorate (optional)

A popular pud in many restaurants is frozen berries with a white chocolate sauce. However, I find that the chocolate sauce sometimes sets too quickly. In my attempt to prevent this from happening, I thought that the sauce would stay hot and gooey for longer if I made the berries warm. Puddings don't get much easier than this.

Hot Berries with Hot White Chocolate Sauce

Timetable: from start to table in 15 minutes
Preparation 5 minutes | Cooking 10 minutes

Bring the cream to the boil in a non-stick saucepan, then remove from the heat and stir in the chocolate until smooth. Fold in the liqueur (if using).

Meanwhile, put all the fruit in another saucepan with the sugar and cordial, and cook over a medium heat. Stir until the berries are warm and have released some of their juices.

Spoon the berries into four large wine glasses, then spoon the chocolate sauce on top.

Antony's tip If you're not a fan of white chocolate, use dark or milk chocolate instead.

Serves 4

150ml (5fl oz) double cream

115g (4oz) white chocolate, broken into small pieces

1 tbsp Amaretto liqueur (optional)

250g (9oz) strawberries, quartered

250g (9oz) blueberries

250g (9oz) raspberries

1 tbsp caster sugar

2 tbsp blackcurrant cordial

Full-On Dairy Pud

This is a cheesecake without the biscuit base but with heaps of dairy fats, which – let's be honest – children need in order to develop strong bones. It tastes delicious and is very quick to make.

Timetable: from start to table in 15 minutes
Preparation 10 minutes │ Cooking 5 minutes

Serves 4

150g (5oz) mascarpone

85g (3oz) ricotta

85g (3oz) icing sugar

Grated zest and juice of
2 limes

240ml (8fl oz) double cream,
whisked to soft peaks

4 shop-bought meringue
nests, broken

225g (8oz) strawberries or
raspberries

2 tbsp grated chocolate, to
decorate

Beat together the mascarpone, ricotta, 55g (2oz) of the icing sugar, lime juice and zest. Blend well, then fold in the double cream and check for sweetness. Fold in the broken meringue.

In a food processor, whizz half the strawberries with the remaining icing sugar, then pass the mixture through a fine sieve to remove the seeds. Slice the remaining strawberries, then fold them into the strawberry compote.

Take four glass tumblers or large wine glasses, spoon the strawberry compote in the bottom of each and top with the lime cheese. Fork up to peaks or smooth flat as you prefer, then top with grated chocolate.

Antony's tip Use different fruit according to what's in season: blackberries, raspberries, apricots… the choice is yours!

Hot Strawberry Custards

If you love berries but want to ring the changes, then this pud ticks all the right boxes. It's quick, it's good value and it looks like you made an effort (but we know different).

Timetable: from start to table in 15 minutes
Preparation 10 minutes | Cooking 5 minutes

Serves 4

450g (1lb) strawberries, quartered

Zest and juice of 1 organic orange

500g (1lb 2oz) tub finest shop-bought fresh custard

3 tbsp caster sugar

Divide the strawberries between four shallow gratin dishes. Sprinkle with a little orange juice and zest, then spoon the custard over the fruit.

Preheat the grill, then sprinkle the custard with the caster sugar. Place under the grill close to the heat source and wait until the sugar has glazed brown; alternatively, use a blowtorch to caramelize the sugar.

Antony's tip This dish is simple and yet incredibly versatile. You can use any fruit that takes your fancy – peaches, raspberries and cooked plums are all great options. And for the grown-ups, a little liqueur mixed into the custard takes this pudding to another dimension.

Mocha Cupcakes

These mocha cupcakes are the perfect way of introducing a slightly more adult taste to your child's food repertoire. Cupcakes are the 'in' thing at the moment.

Timetable: from start to table in 35 minutes
Preparation 10 minutes | Cooking 20–25 minutes, plus cooling

Preheat the oven to 180°C/360°F/Gas 4.

In a food mixer or by hand, beat together the sugar and butter until pale – about 5 minutes. Dissolve the coffee in the boiling water, then beat it into the butter mix. Beat in the eggs one at a time, then fold in the flour and mix briefly until combined.

Line a muffin tray with paper cake cases, then divide the mixture equally between the cases, which should be about three-quarter full. Bake in the oven for 20–25 minutes, until risen and the sponge springs back when pushed. Allow to cool.

For the icing, dissolve the cocoa powder in the boiling water, then add to the mascarpone along with the icing sugar and beat until combined. Spoon or pipe the icing onto the top of the cupcakes and sprinkle with grated chocolate.

Antony's tip Grown-ups might want to add a dash of their favourite liqueur.

Makes 12

FOR THE CUPCAKES

200g (7oz) caster sugar

200g (7oz) unsalted butter, softened

2 tsp espresso-strength coffee granules

1 tbsp boiling water

4 free-range eggs

200g (7oz) self-raising flour

FOR THE ICING

1 tbsp cocoa powder

1 tbsp boiling water

250g (9oz) tub mascarpone

2 tbsp icing sugar

Grated chocolate, to decorate

Index

Acknowledgements

There are too many people to thank but certain individuals deserve a special mention:

To my fantastic wife, Jacinta, and our two children, Toby and Billie, who suffered from my lack of quality time yet supported me throughout as I managed to juggle my time plus everything else going on in my life.

To Nicola Atherton, my energetic and ultra-efficient PA, who fielded hundreds of phone calls from the publishers and was regularly on hand to smooth troubled waters when the pressures of deadlines occasionally took their toll.

To Fiona Lindsay and Mary Bekhait at Limelight Management who are always there to make sure I have more than enough work to handle.

To my great staff at my restaurants and Food And Wine To Go: Notting Grill, Kew Grill, The Greyhound Free House & Grill and The Lamb at Satwell, Barnes Grill, Windsor Grill and the latest addition, Windsor Larder.

To David Wilby, friend, business partner and Operations Director who successfully keeps the restaurants and shop afloat in my absences.

To the various friends who unwittingly tested some of the recipes over the long boozy lunches that we held over the last year.

And finally to Rebecca Spry and her team at Mitchell Beazley, for giving me the opportunity to produce this cook book and turning my offerings into a beautifully executed book, and also to Deidre Rooney whose wonderful photography made all the dishes look so temptingly delicious.